For She Who Grieves:

Practical Wisdom for Living Hope

With

Amy Hooper Hanna

and

Holly Joy McIlwain

Aurora Corialis Publishing

Pittsburgh, PA

For She Who Grieves: Practical Wisdom for Living Hope

Printed in the United States of America

Edited by: Cori Wamsley, Aurora Corialis Publishing

Cover Design: Karen Captline, BetterBe Creative

Paperback ISBN: 978-1-958481-99-8

Ebook ISBN: 978-1-958481-98-1

Praise for *For She Who Grieves*

"Our nature of existence can be shattered in a moment when grief enters. Whether you have a story or know someone who does, this book will help you find a way to embrace grief and rise above. The collection of stories is not simply profound; it is the love that is written in the words by Amy and Holly that surround the stories that is the heartfelt hug. You immediately feel at home as if listening to friends and want to support the women who so bravely stepped forward to share their stories so others could be braver. A must read for anyone whose heart is open and willing to learn about loving their grief to heal their soul."

~ PJ Jackson | Chief Empowerment Officer, Founder, and CEO of Positive Knowledge, LLC and Author of *The Labyrinth Influence, Awaken the Wisdom Within*

~*~

"Pure-hearted and thoughtfully written. A true companion guide for your heart and soul! With wide-open honesty, vulnerability and care, Amy and Holly accomplish the goal of bringing together both tenderness and tools for the grief, love, and hope in us all."

~ Rachel Madorsky, LCSW, Bestselling Author of *How to Love Yourself In Less Than a Week and Also for the Rest of Your Life*

~*~

"Grief, like life, is a journey of self-discovery, growth, and working through layers of conditioning; in this book, Amy and Holly inspire and empower others to experience their organic truth, gain greater wisdom and self-awareness, and live in hope and joy along the way. Speaking their minds and hearts along with the voices of many others, they reveal a huge capacity for connection. *For She Who Grieves: Practical Wisdom for Living Hope* compassionately and respectfully supports and activates the healing potential of others."

~Juliette Stapleton | Online Visibility Strategist, Marketing By Human Design Expert

~*~

"Divorce from a spouse. Death of a parent. Estrangement from a family member. Disillusionment with a dream. While the causes of our grief are common, our reactions are not. Through *For She Who Grieves*, Amy and Holly share practical wisdom about mourning, yet living in hope. Thank you for this timely take on surviving loss with grace.

~ Lisa Patten | Founder, Dandelion Communications, Author of *Say Smart Stuff*

~*~

"*For She Who Grieves* is an in-depth look into grief and how it can affect every aspect of our lives. This book is a must read for anyone experiencing grief or anyone who knows someone who is. We all experience grief at some point in our lives, and it helps to know that our feelings, whatever they may be, are valid and normal, even if they don't feel normal.

"As a bereaved mother, I can relate to so much in this book, especially the feeling of finding myself in unfamiliar territory. Amy and Holly did a fabulous job explaining grief, navigating through the unfamiliar territory of grief and showing how you can rise above the darkness to find light and hope."

Dana Ziemniak | Author of *Blue is the Color of Heaven: The Story of a Boy's Love, Strength, & Beyond*

The Fine Print

Much of this book is based on contributors' stated, written, or published personal stories and experiences, recollections, notes, and journal entries. Due to the sensitivity of the material, stories have been parsed into sections, and some information has been modified out of respect for anonymity and to protect the identities of those involved. Please dismiss any similarities or inferences to unnamed people; assumption is dangerous, and judgment is not the point.

The events and dialogue in contributor stories are approximations of what took place, what was actually said or relayed. Contributors acknowledge there is more than one side to every story—this is their own. They realize that not everyone will like their truth or accept it as their own, hope for peace for whoever may be unintentionally hurt or harmed by their story as they tell it, and trust in the rightness of sharing it.

The authors and contributors are offering their own personal perspectives on the experience of grief and how it relates to hope and joy. It is our intention that sharing these stories will help people find their peace and the fortitude to see them through the days ahead. In our experience, healing, hope, and wisdom spring from openness. These stories prompt our reflections, while raising human consciousness and connection.

This book is not intended to offer legal or psychological advice nor should it be used for that purpose. The author and contributors are not responsible for personal decisions based on the subject matter contained in this book. You are advised to seek professional assistance in your area of residence with individuals who are qualified in the subject matter contained in this book.

This book reminds us that others grieve in much the same way as we; taking responsibility for our lives and nurturing ourselves and renewing our energy is critical, as we journey forth bravely one day, hesitantly the next. It's a solo journey, yet interestingly we make it together. In writing this, we have grown even more appreciative of our grief and our scars and are grateful to share it with you.

Table of Contents

Letters from Amy & Holly

~*~

From Amy ...

I'm the type of person who would be interested in how many hours were spent writing this book. And you know what? I can't tell you.

Unlike my line of work, where I've been documenting every 15 minutes of my time for over 30 years, not to mention dotting every "i" and crossing every "t," this was a labor of love. Don't get me wrong, I love my work, it's just that this book came from me at a time when I was done. Mentally and emotionally done, both personally and professionally, with justifying every detail. Done with the pressure to meet burdensome demands and others' expectations, done with scheduling every minute of my day. Tired of speaking up, seeking alternatives, speaking loudly, and my voice not being heard. Ignored. Tired of feeling powerless because of other people's bullshit. Because of my own bullshit.

After the grief, trials, tribulations, and transformations experienced among the joys in my own life, I made an organic, and conscious, decision to only go with what lights me up and carve out the bullshit I was putting up with from others, that I was essentially putting up with myself. I wanted to risk it—risk just saying, "No more. I'm done with that," and move on to what I trust will be a crazy good thing.

Could I financially afford to just listen more to my heart, act more in line with my soul? Nope! But something was telling me it was worth the risk. Scratch that—I FELT that it would be worth the risk. Actually, I knew I couldn't afford to NOT risk doing that. I was at a place where I was just plain done experiencing grief and having to constantly manage my response to other people's actions. It affected my emotional, mental, and physical health. Deep down, I knew I was losing the battle. I was so tired. That's not to say that I gave up all responsibility. Heck no. I pride myself on being the best mom, worker, friend, family member I can be. Because I care. About me. You. About people. Souls.

I am so grateful for the great friends and family that I have, who have always been there for me, whether I reached out or not. And provided the original space for me to start accepting my truth. Whether they knew my story or not. Whether we talk every day or every few months or even years. If you wonder if I might be talking about you, I am! I trust you, and I love you. You bring joy to my world in good times and bad!

Holly and the Brave Women Project became a part of my life at the right time, for a reason. I don't think anyone anticipated the vulnerability and authenticity that quickly surfaced in that group. Granted, with a focus on bravery, I guess it's natural that the personal side emerges. But it was highly intelligent, motivated, driven women networking in a (virtual) space that encouraged what we apparently all needed most—to be REAL. Not just with friends, but essentially strangers. Because Holly is profound, she created something profound: a place to escape from the bullshit, consciously support each other instead of unconsciously compete, and make connections that have more personal and practical rippling benefits than we can count.

So. BWP is the space where I started voicing my truth beyond my immediate circle. Risked sharing my personal story ... that was essentially part of me professionally. Risked sharing my grief, and in doing so, realized the value of hearing other people's stories. Understanding other women's sadness and joy. For gaining hope. Perspective. Objectivity. Understanding. Compassion. Connection.

Collecting these stories has been an incredible honor.

It is said that an invisible red thread connects those who are destined to meet, regardless of time, place or circumstance. The thread may stretch or tangle, but it will never break. This message was on a card tied to a small bell with a fine, red ribbon, handed out at my sister-in-law's celebration of life. *"Everyone here was and continues to be connected to mom's red thread,"* wrote my niece. "*I hope that when you look at this piece of red ribbon you remember how thankful and grateful she was to have her thread connect with yours."*

I hope that when you read this book, you feel a connection to my red thread.

With love, kindness, and gratitude,

Amy Hooper Hanna

P.S. As to how many hours I spent on this book? Just the right amount.

Dedicated in loving memory to Elisabeth Perrault Hooper

04/11/1967 – 03/03/2021

Grieved, loved, celebrated.

~*~

From Holly ...

Sorting through grief is really hard.

Really freaking hard.

I remember the moment when this book started to move through me. I was lying in bed. I had just suffered a loss that changed me forever. I didn't know what to do with my grief, so I decided to share it. I kept it private at first, until I understood how I was changing, and then slowly and carefully, I revealed my grief to people who were brave enough to love me through it.

Eventually, I learned that grief moves ... first like the flutter of early pregnancy ... and then does barrel rolls like each of my sons did after 20 weeks, into the stillness. Finally, grief rolled over and through my entire body, demanding to be birthed. Odd, isn't it? Experiencing grief and sharing this book was so much like the spark that started it—and so heartbreakingly different. The grief of our miscarriage opened up my heart and friendships to make space for hope.

So often, people feel strange about speaking to grief. I hope that this book allows women to experience grief differently. Sometimes there are no words to say. But sometimes there are. I wish someone would have handed me this book and a box of chocolates earlier. For she who grieves needs a friend to wait with. Wait for healing. Wait for the hurting to ease. Wait for the hope to grow.

Collecting the stories of the women we mention in this book was obviously so hard. Amy and I shed tears for them, with them, and together. Amy and I shed tears silently, alone, as we worked through the finer points. We desired so much to tell stories and share the points of view in one voice, never allowing for one of us, or any of the women we learned from, to grieve alone. **For she who grieves with one voice is speaking to all of us.**

As the founder of Brave Women Project, a high-impact not-for-profit that serves women who often feel the pressure of doing it all, all at once, all the time, it was important to point to the women in the community who built us up. The wisdom and support that we received from the professional development sessions, from our Brave Women Brunches, the speakers, and mostly from each other in the "Come As You Are" support circles needed to be captured. One million "thank yous" to the women who shared their hearts with us formally and informally. Every page of this book includes their watermark.

This book has changed me. I've walked with grief for many miles now. Because of this book, I look at my sons and my husband differently. Listening to other people's losses has caused me to love more deeply in my own home. I want to be a more grateful person. I want to be a more compassionate person. I want to be a more courageous person—standing with others in their grief and also, sometimes, sitting down with them too. Hell, falling to the floor with them even.

Writing this book also caused me to think more about one loss that hurt differently because too many things remained unsaid, too much time went by. When I received the phone call that relayed the unbelievable news that one of my sweetest friends had suddenly and unexpectedly passed, I was dumbstruck. Then I learned she was also halfway through her fifth pregnancy. Attending the funeral, saying goodbye to my friend, seeing her children and bereaved husband, grieving with her family, and praying for strength for everyone involved was, and remains, one of the most difficult moments of my adult life. She's been on my mind and in my heart, prompting me along through these pages.

There's no secret to moving from grief to hope. There's not. But there are hundreds of movements that we can choose in allowing grief to accompany us rather than fight it. I hope that offers hope to our readers.

When *For She Who Leads*, my first book, came out, I was excited and proud. It was through that book launch that I was introduced to Amy Hooper Hanna. I knew we'd stay connected — she was brilliant and funny, and we were in similar industries. I never guessed that we'd build a community of women and write a book that has the capacity to save people's heart-lives like this. So today, as I write this and we give *For She Who Grieves* to the world, I'm nervous. Changing heart-lives is big work, and I don't think we'll get much rest after this. Thanks Amy, for saying "yes" to this crazy journey and for working with me. Thanks also to the many people who listened to concepts, talked through pain, and held my hand.

Holly McIlwain

Dedicated in loving memory to Sarah Shulzetenberg Harkins

08/02/1981 – 07/28/2014.

Grieved, treasured, missed.

Foreword

I am asking my friend about her experience with grief for this book I'm writing, when she states, *"I've been living with a secret.*

"It's not a total secret. Over time, I've shared my story with enough confidants that I feel I've spoken my truth to some degree. Yet there's a part of me that still wriggles uncomfortably, like I haven't spoken my truth WHOLLY. Not because I haven't shared all the details, but because the experience is a part of me that most people don't know, even some important people very close to me."

She's both a private and open person, so I'm not surprised by this. I know transparency and honesty are essential values of hers, and she promotes those in her children. Integrity, kindness and respect are huge for her. So is protection and loyalty. I know she has been through a lot, but I'm not sure exactly what.

"This particular story of grief is a tricky story to tell, because the grief is over the demise of my ethereal spirit. It involves guilty others and impacts innocent ones and is muddled with the duality of obvious uncertainties and hidden truths, of lots of gray among the black and white. Uncovering the hard reality is not always easy. Yet truth is important to me, and hearing other people's true stories has been essential to my moving through grief."

I could see why she had remained torn in sharing her story. I was intrigued, perplexed, afraid, and honored all at the same time.

"This is MY story. This is MY experience. It should be heard. And here's how I will tell it..."

~*~

Life is filled with millions of moments that tell a story.

1,320,000,000 minutes in fact, if you are fortunate enough to live to be 80 years old. Say that number out loud: One billion. One billion, three hundred twenty million. In any one minute of those 1,320,000,000 moments, we may be either alone or lonely, healthy and happy, hurting or hopeful, mourning or mystified, or perhaps even just at peace. There will be moments of joy, and there will be moments of pain. Loss is a part of life.

Some believe that it's only appropriate to grieve certain things. But your loss, whatever it may be, is personal; how you feel is how you feel, and there's no shame in that. If the person, pet, relationship, or object was significant to you, it's normal to feel strongly, even conflicted, about the loss you're experiencing. Whatever the cause or context of your suffering, there are ways to ease your pain and help you live with your loss and come to terms with it. In time, you will find new meaning and eventually move in the present toward your future and feel joy in your life.

Perhaps one of these scenarios resonates with you:

"Parenting remotely is excruciating both personally and practically. Being instinctively tethered to your child doesn't release just because they are at their father's home."

"Choosing something because it's good doesn't make it any easier to not choose something that is not good for me."

"Being a motherless child is the most unnatural thing in the world. Especially if your mother is still living."

"Building a home is the American dream, becoming a family is what we were raised to do. Saying goodbye to a place and a life is a grief felt at the molecular level. Every part of that home had my DNA all over it."

"Burying the father of my child shouldn't happen before his first birthday."

"Losing my life savings, my retirement, my ability to pay the mortgage—in one day—didn't seem possible. Yet here I am."

"I'm ashamed to admit that I'm grieving. Is it selfish for me to grieve, when my partner is the one who is suffering?"

"It took me a year to say I'm grieving the man I married. And now I'm confronted with the man I'm married to."

"In hindsight, I have always wondered if I should have called the psychiatric unit or the police that night. It crossed my mind at the time when he threatened suicide,

but I was scared he would never forgive me for putting him in a psychiatric unit or causing a scene with the neighbors."

"Women are supposed to have breasts. Cancer isn't supposed to take them away. Not only am I battling this disease; I'm battling myself when I look in the mirror."

"I didn't want to fight anymore. So I packed what I could, which wasn't much, and then I left."

"When we lost another baby, I didn't think I could go on."

"If you have any concept of physical, sexual, psychological, mental, or emotional abuse and what it does to a person, you will understand that it is a brutal attack on your mind, your heart, your psyche—the very precious essence of life. The grief that befalls is dark, dense and durable. Truly devastating."

You may not find your exact scenario or story here, but you will find your moments in the stories that were offered to us. Pieces will hit close to home. Your story is unique, just like everyone's experience with grief is different. Your story is incredible. Can you imagine the tome this would be if we regaled all the scenarios we're aware of, let alone not aware of, being grieved among family and friends, not to mention their children?

Here, by sharing some very personal and sensitive stories, relevant research and tried tactics, we aim to help everyone who is touched by grief. Despite any similarity to a horror movie, and in some places a dark comedy (we do try to lighten up at times), here you will find soul, richness, and meaning. The sensitive stories offered are ones that provide awareness and deeper understanding of complex situations and show us there are healthy ways to ease the pain, experience joy, and emerge ... well, better.

We are not here to diagnose, we're here to discover. Or maybe "uncover" is a better word. In sharing grief, in hearing stories, we see ourselves. Hopefully, you will uncover something helpful, if not for you, someone else. Peace, comfort, belief, and relief can be found on the road between Shitsville and Joytown.

"To love at all is to be vulnerable. Love anything, and your heart will be wrung and possibly broken. If you want to make sure of keeping it intact you must give it to no one, not even an animal. Wrap it carefully round with hobbies and little luxuries; avoid all entanglements. Lock it up safe in the casket or coffin of your selfishness. But in that casket, safe, dark, motionless, airless, it will change. It will not be broken; it will become unbreakable, impenetrable, irredeemable. To love is to be vulnerable."

C.S. Lewis, *The Four Loves*

Introduction

For She Who Grieves...

"I felt the significance of grief most remarkably when I collapsed face down on my bed, utterly exhausted, alone and hopeless, and a solid, deep, guttural moan emerged from somewhere in my body. My grief was so primal, strong, and sad..."

Ahhh, grief. We all know it as overwhelming sadness. Profound sorrow. Deep distress. Desperate emotional anguish. Keen mental suffering. Grief is the process we go through that includes a whole host of emotions and thoughts we feel on the inside, when we experience significant loss, end, or change. Mourning is how we express that grief outwardly. Suffering is what we do. It all sucks. Figuratively, and literally; it can suck the life right out of your soul.

Put in the simplest terms, grief is an intense emotional experience triggered by a loss. While commonly associated with death, grief can occur anytime reality is not what we wanted, hoped for, or expected (Stanaway, 2020). It can be experienced in situations like divorce, separation, injury, illness, material destruction, or bankruptcy, to name a few. Lesser known considerations are when there is loss of trust, approval, safety, faith, or control.

Many books have been written on grief and how to adjust to loss. **This is a book about tending to pain with care. It's about the evolution that can come from suffering, the change that transpires from challenge. It's about good grief.** We don't profess to be experts. Yet, through the personal stories and research we've collected, we have learned there is much power and practical wisdom to be found in the journey from sadness to joy, from suffering to relief.

What you're about to read weaves together the experiences, thoughts, research, and whispers of a group of women who are brave enough to approach grief, and caring enough to share it. It may be hard to detect a single voice here, and we intended it that way. Grief is intensely personal, while at the same time, it is incredibly communal. The stories, the raw emotion, the carefully constructed commentary, serve a purpose. A very serious one: **For those of us who search for relief from grief, we propose a reframe.**

~*~

Grief can be a difficult and uncomfortable experience.

Grief may even be traumatic.

What if we focused on grief as something that helps us grow wiser and more resilient,

Rather than something that breaks and damages?

Our position is to embrace grief rather than reject it.

We are not denying the pain that comes from and with grief.

We are advocating that in grief there is growth.
The experience of pain is valid. Your experience of pain is valid.

Not all pain is negative.
Childbirth, for example, is painful and even sometimes traumatic,
But it brings a new life and opportunity for love and connection into the world.
Grief can be experienced as gestation for new life and opportunity

For love and connection, For hope and joy,
For she who grieves.

~ h & a

~*~

Part 1

Chapter 1: Good Mourning

"Grief is the price we pay for love."

~ Queen Elizabeth II, Former Queen of the United Kingdom

A Limited History of Mourning

Did you know that there was a period of time known as "The Golden Age of Mourning"? Queen Victoria, Former Queen of the United Kingdom of Great Britain and Ireland, widowed at a relatively young age in 1861, spent much of her public life in mourning. The Victorian era modeled mourning after the presentation of the monarch, and the reality of shorter life expectancy marketed death and mourning as part of living. Human interactions were marked by losses–nearly half of all children didn't make it to teen years, childbirth commonly resulted in death of one or both participants, industrial and farm conditions were less than safe, and travel was limited to highly vulnerable methods. Life was hard, and death was likely. To live was to die, and to love was to mourn. Mourning was not shameful, but social. The religious rituals, symbolism, and even superstitions threaded cultural and societal practices, providing punctuation marks on mourning.

There are some theories in the psychology community that suggest that historical grief practices that involved the whole community were more psychologically healthy than the more isolated contemporary practices. Public expressions of grief provide a release for the grieving, and remind observers of their own mortality, as well as alert the community that someone is suffering amongst them.

Looking back further in history, the elaborate preparation of the body by ancient Egyptian people marked the journey from the living world to and through the afterlife. Coupled with the evolution from wicker basket to sarcophagi, the familiar tombs still existing today serve as a commanding reminder of the power in death. Traditional Irish and Scottish "keening," loudly wailing for the dead, gave voice to the gutting experience of grief that has been described over and over again by the grieving. In Ancient Rome, family members paraded through town wearing wax models made directly from the face of the deceased as a mask to remember and honor the loss. Grief and celebration—ritually and hopefully—push the human experience and expression of grief into the searchlight and out of the dark. For she who grieves, thoroughly experiencing ALL OF IT allows for healing, hope, and her story to be what it is.

HerStory of Mourning

"While grief is unique to each of us as individuals, it is also a shared, universal human experience. The last two years have seen loss on an unprecedented scale and changed the

way grief is felt and experienced on all levels. The time to talk about grief is now."

~ Hospice of Southern Maine

Grief is experienced by all humans, everywhere, though everyone's own story of grief is deeply personal, usually painful, and incredibly intimate. Grief is not just experienced as a part of death, but in other significant losses—jobs, body parts, health, even a loss of self. Failure, violence, accidents, trauma, sickness, pandemics, forces of nature ... all create environments fertile for grief.

Experts on grief, such as Russell Friedman, co-founder of the Grief Recovery Institute, and Cole James, executive director of the Institute, describe "stress" as another word for "grief," explaining that the result of the conflicting feelings caused by the end of or change in a familiar pattern of behavior and natural reaction to any change that occurs in life is, in fact, a stressful experience (Moeller, 2017). Stress-filled, and stressful. Stress, as we know, is something that is manageable. Stress, as we have experienced, is something that will demand a response if left unchecked, and our research has shown us that grief has this similar reaction. Grief demands a response. However, more patiently and quietly than the stress of daily life and work.

Grief—this natural response to loss, this experience of suffering on an emotional level, in the wake of something or someone deeply loved having been taken away—sucks. Told ya. Grief is what we think and feel on the inside when we experience loss of any kind, particularly the death of one we care for. Examples of these emotions include fear, loneliness, panic, pain, yearning, anxiety, emptiness, etc. These experiences often carry a heavy feeling with them, relating back to the origin of the word "grief," in French, which means "to burden." This internal meaning and emotional burden given to the experience of loss helps us to understand why grief feels heavy sometimes.

Grief is a very broad topic, covering many kinds of losses and an incredible range of emotions, so a single definition of "grief" can be difficult to capture. The difficult and unexpected emotions which bubble, blister, and weep subsequent to an experience of loss can feel overwhelming. While grief is internal, the voluntary, and sometimes involuntary, expression of these emotions demonstrates the act of mourning. The intentional behaviors associated with grieving, such as paying respects, sitting shiva, weeping, memorializing the loss, and so many more activities unique to each circumstance and culture are more familiar means of mourning. Mourning, however, is the outward expression of grief, and can be at the same time difficult to detect AND difficult to conceal.

Whether we realize it or not, our grief, pain, and sorrow, to whatever degree it is being experienced, is felt by others. They may not be able to put their finger on it. Hell, we may not be able to put our finger on it in ourselves. It's an energy that soaks in and seeps out. The veil that exists when grief is shrouded affects our transparency and authenticity. And the division widens. The grief deepens. The isolation suffocates. This is a conversation for she who grieves, a conversation about the way that women can walk through and work through grief together, but we cannot do the work for another.

We know we can't always control our environment and what happens. We can, however, control how we respond. For the most part. In many circumstances, we can make choices and respond, but in some experiences, involuntary responses to grief appear, and wading out of them can be just as overwhelming. Our response is greatly influenced by our life experience and mindset (and the reverse is true as well). With some knowledge, perspective, introspection, and discipline, we can change our response (and life).

Like any challenge, grief will either build you or break you. It's your choice. Again, for the most part. A person's life experience deeply impacts the ability to release and work through grief. Our education, environment, and personal lived experiences set the course of behaviors and experiences that are comfortable and create a sense of psychological security, even if those behaviors ultimately are not healthy. The recognition of the present place and time that grief emerges presents the opportunity to pursue hope, or sink into hopelessness.

For She Who Grieves...

"There is a light within you. Within each of us. Others may see it, but only you can hold your own. For some of us, it's covered with layers of gunk and muck. But it's there. It may take a lot of digging. A lot of heavy crap is likely heaped on top. It may take a considerable amount of time. Friends might try to help you. But. You have to have the will to dig yourself out. Will or rot. There's really nothing

else to do. At least start. Rinse the dust away with your tears. Dig for the light. The treasure. It's there. Be patient. You will uncover it. The gold you find inside is so worth it in the end."

In times of heightened emotion and the *stress* of grief, the dynamic between the independent thought and the regressive behavior becomes palpable. At this point, a choice exists: to give grief the space it deserves, or to squeeze grief into a small box and tuck it away.

The growing field of death workers, individuals trained in both social work and hospital systems, while honoring the intentions and needs of individuals seeking "a good death," presses firmly against the advance of modern medicine and the temptation to sterilize death and over-medicate grief, steering all involved away from the uncomfortable feelings as much as possible. Death doula and palliative care social worker Tanisha Bowman, explains, "I believe in a good death. But the definition is different for everyone. For me, it's the best death they can have with the resources they have available. The reality of death, even a good death, isn't always anything that someone expects."

Bowman also shares, "A person's death is not just *their* death." Powerful words for those of us left behind and looking ahead. For she who grieves, hope is holding on to the hands of history and pulling another person along through the story.

The behaviors of grief that were somewhat necessary and culturally ritualistic in generations before us helped people to hold space while growing both stronger and closer from the shared experiences. These practices weren't perfect, and were messier than what many of us are comfortable with today. We aren't proposing a complete reverse course and return to the Victorian era, but we are hoping to cast a glow on grief and mourning that allows for she who grieves to exhale and take up a bit of space for herself. The grief practices of men and women differ, as do many of the behaviors, thought patterns, and social interactions.

Grief has been part of the human experience forever, regardless of culture, age or gender. Of course, there are some noted differences among certain demographics, but in the grand scheme of things, there's relatively little research and much to be understood about grief. In some cultures, crying is not as accepted, while wailing is in others. A child may be more likely to grieve a sentimental material object than an adult would. Women may gain more from social support from other women, than men do beyond their wives. Regardless of any statistical differences, grief touches us all.

Consider the work of women inside the home and the family unit. One might observe that the (endless) required activities prevent stillness and time for mourning; rather, processing of grief is often tangled up with loads of laundry, people to feed, and persons to care for. As women have stepped outside the home in droves to be successful in the workplace, the acts of caregiving and homemaking haven't necessarily fallen away. We hear (and have experienced personally) the problem: we don't have time to grieve in the way we need or even want to when there are children to feed. Bills to pay. Laundry to fold. Work to do. Often, women experience love by doing, and for that reason, slowing down to move through grief can be put off and delayed.

This sense of responsibility supersedes the actual biological need to process grief. You read that right. There is an *actual biological need to process grief.* This need to grieve stems from the connection we have with that which is lost (or left, as you will read). The connection that once existed has binding (or bonding) capabilities, and disconnecting is a healthy action as separation is experienced. By un-bonding to one thing, we become free to bond to another. After a loss, especially a traumatic loss, it is difficult to move forward until grief is processed and experienced. Holding space for grief is critical, since there's no clear timeline for moving through the stages of grief and finding hope.

Women in particular don't always get permission from themselves to hold space for grief. The notion of "permission" is a sticking point for the authors of this book—we are beyond any point in history that required women to seek permission for anything. However, a person's background, family of origin, and lived experiences all influence their need for permission or reversion back to a place where seeking permission is a reaction rather than choice. We've learned that creating a space to grieve, in solitude or in community, brings about healing and hope more efficiently than denial and despondency. But, it is easier to sanitize grief or shove it in a box.

Common in some parts of our Western culture is the immediate removal of the deceased by a funeral director, or movement to the morgue. Death professionals manage all the details of care and preparation of the body, and family members get to "visit" with the dead and each other for quaint two-hour periods and then perhaps attend a religious service or memorial and then a burial. Typically this is followed by a funeral lunch (or wake). It's all very sterile and prescriptive. Anecdotally, we hear that this experience is more exhausting for the grieving than helpful, and prolongs the journey from grief to hope.

There are certainly religions and cultures and positions in the West that are less sterile and prescriptive, that make death more about a celebration of life, with joyful music, happy memories, and fond stories shared among family and friends and even strangers. We know this kind of experience is more energizing, helpful, and hopeful for the grieving. You may even walk out feeling better than when you walked in. Just think of the New Orleans Jazz Funerals–a community wide procession with music, family, and friends is strictly ritualized, but with a different tone. The "second line" follows the brass band, and they are not solemn at all. They move with the music, marching and dancing, seeming to "rejoice" at death and the promise of eternal life for Christians.

Looking at the more systematic approach to funerals may cause one to wonder if it is more about ritually ending grief and mourning with a stopping point, than a time and place to share, embrace and encourage grief to be felt. With grief unresolved, hope becomes stifled. For those of us anchored to our unresolved grief, we have to take into account the life experiences, lived experience and present place for she who grieves.

Value in Mourning

Dying is the easy part. Being left behind to wade through the logistics of dying is difficult. With significant loss, a lot of people would be satisfied with coping or surviving. We don't think this book is for just "survivors." It's deeper than that. It's not for people who are simply content coping with a difficult situation or who are comfortable complaining or seeing a victim when they look in the mirror.

Here's why: the label "survivor" indicates victimhood in some sense, and keeps us stuck in rocks and mud, which inhibits greater growth. The stories in this book are from women who have experienced or attended to grief from various forms of traumatic events and layers of loss stemming not only from death and dying, but from disease, divorce, destruction, and abuse, to name a few. This book is not about being a *victim*, but about being a *victor*. It's about HOPE—to borrow a spiritual teacher's acronym: *Helping Other People get Enlightened* (Orloff, 2010).

This is a book for people who are brave, who are fighters, who want to engage. People who want to bounce back, up, and over from deflation. Who want to reclaim or regain their life and soul after significant loss. Who want to understand and accept what they cannot change and use that as fuel to test and change what they can to propel forward. This book is for warriors. Warriors have a will not only to survive, but to thrive. Warriors use the mud and rocks in clever ways to build up their bunker and stock artillery to battle whatever battle they are facing. For she who grieves, the battle for good grief is being won.

What good exists in mourning? Lots of it, if you know where to look.

Professor of English and folklore studies Daniel Wojcik, and colleague Robert Dobler, lecturer of folklore, believe that there is great value in the rituals around mourning:

By doing things in a culturally defined way—by performing the same acts as ancestors have done—ritual participants engage in venerated traditions to connect with something enduring and eternal. Rituals make boundaries between life and death, the sacred and the profane, memory and experience, permeable. The dead seem less far away and less forgotten. Death itself becomes more natural and familiar. (Dobbler and Wojcik, 2017)

The Day of the Dead celebration joins together the practice of mourning with the purpose of remembrance. Dia De Los Muertos (Day of the Dead) marks three days of intentionality around mourning and the mystery of the afterlife, publicly and intimately in the homes of family members. The loss of rituals like this throughout the world and over time has not only snuffed out the celebration of life, but also stifled the expressions of grief that may be considered cathartic and necessary in the healing process.

Contrasting with the public practices of grief of ancient to Victorian times, the ramifications of the most recent global pandemic further displaced acknowledgement of death and communal mourning. Yes, the awareness of mortality and body counts was present, but the ability to grieve together was limited.

Perhaps people of Jewish descent have it right. *Shiva* is a Hebrew word that is used to remind people to sit and be with. It is a period of time (seven days to be exact) with designated and formalized mourning by the immediate family of the deceased. The beauty of *shiva* is that the community comes to sit with those who are mourning. They can't do anything to fix it. They can't make it go away. But they can be with. Being with another person in their pain is enough. There doesn't need to be conversation. There doesn't need to be entertainment. There doesn't need to be noise. There just needs to be. The moments existing in *shiva* allow for people to just be. And those moments matter.

Why did we write this book? Well, the authors of this book became part of a movement "to do one brave thing every day," which revealed a series of tender stories that women have been carrying for generations. In carrying these stories, and quietly sharing them, women have been grieving in silence. Why? Women have to keep it together for everyone else.

In the book *One Year After: From Grief to Hope*, Elly Sheykhet gives voice to something so raw and untamed that it opened up a whole new view on the role of grief and the act of grieving:

> I felt so much pain, anger, disappointment, and surprisingly, shame. Some unexplainable type of embarrassment made me feel very awkward. I did not feel like myself anymore. I felt like I had lost my identity and that the people at work would judge me. I felt like a failure of a mother, one who has

> allowed her daughter to be taken in such an unimaginable way. I felt very guilty for being unable to save my child's life, but I fought these feelings aggressively. (Sheykhet, 2020)

Do women need permission to grieve? Absolutely not. But here's the thing: Even if intellectually we know that permission is not needed, somehow the speed of life and the weight of responsibilities takes priority over sitting with grief and allowing time to help us heal. But time doesn't heal all wounds on its own. It's likely that we actually have to do some of the work. Not to get OVER grief. One never gets OVER grief. But in going through it, the majority of women may need a nudge, if not outright permission. That's why a partner was significant for this book ... and a network of women who championed our bravery to go to places that we hadn't been ready or wanting to go to before.

We discovered an intensity, a voice in one's head that whispers self-imposed guidelines and expectations that are not always fair to the person experiencing grief. We wanted to create some space for she who grieves to begin by accepting that we all have been, and many of us are, in a place of grief.

Take a moment to think about your first experience and encounter of grief.

How was grief modeled to you as a child?

What were the grief practices that were customary in your family of origin and community?

How did these things evolve as you matured?

What were the things that you found yourself grieving in childhood, early adolescence, and as a young adult?

What are the things that you have grieved since?

What grief practices have you adopted?

What grief is with you now?

What grief remains unacknowledged?

What if the experience of grief brings relief?

Feel the Hope

Get yourself some flowers and acknowledge that embracing grief doesn't have to be filled with sadness. The flowers will fill your space with color, scent, and a reminder that yes, while all beautiful things will end, they can be celebrated fully. Some hypoallergenic ideas: hydrangeas, carnations, sunflowers, peonies, roses, tulips, orchids, daffodils, and irises!

Chapter 2: Never Enough Time to Say Goodbye

"Grief is overwhelming and one of the most painful emotions any human will ever encounter. While the pain of grief is the same whether the death is sudden or anticipated, a sudden loss is shocking and disorienting, reducing our ability to cope with and understand what has happened."

~ Regan Olsson

Unfortunately, many of us have experienced the disorientation that accompanies a sudden loss.

Johns Hopkins defines sudden loss as:

[...] a death that happens unexpectedly and suddenly, like a fatal accident or heart attack. Such tragedies can leave survivors feeling shocked and confused. Loved ones are often left with many questions, unresolved issues, and a range of emotions, including anger, guilt, and pain. Support from family, friends, and clergy is important to people experiencing sudden loss. (Grief and Loss, 2019)

For She Who Grieves ...

"I remember thinking if I could just RUN and RUN I could outrun my dad's death. That once I got to some destination, he wouldn't really be gone. Then my sister became physically ill, collapsing in my hallway. Sudden death messes with you."

Research shows that the impact that sudden loss has on an individual can include decreased immunity, cardiovascular irregularities, psychological impairments, depression and anxiety, and increased morbidity (Fagundes, 2020). Loss can literally make us sick. While the brain is constructed to protect itself and the body it runs, the sympathetic and parasympathetic nervous systems have calculated responses to sudden loss and grief.

Why does this matter? Because when we don't have enough time to say goodbye or grieve properly, we should expect that our body and brain will insist that we start to process.

So, job losses, home losses, marriage losses, deaths, illnesses, children leaving or changing, futures shifting or folding, bankruptcy, infertility, broken relationships, whatever it is ... each has the right to hold space and be grieved. In fact, each requires us to step back, pay attention, and grieve properly, whatever that is.

As She Grieves ...

"When her husband was diagnosed with multiple sclerosis, it came at a really bad time. 'Is there ever a good time for a diagnosis like that?' she asked. They had lost so much already and fought to get to a good place in their marriage and with their family. They spent hours talking

about the life they would have together, raising the kids, playing baseball in the backyard, traveling, retiring. When the diagnosis came, it felt like their future was stolen from them and they hadn't a prayer to change it. And her grief had to get tucked away as they navigated specialists and treatments and the cascade of bad news.

Their life would never be what they hoped. He wouldn't be the partner she needed. She wasn't allowed to be upset, she told herself. She confesses that sitting in denial and anger and bargaining for a long time felt more like a hamster wheel that she couldn't get off. There was too much to do, constantly. Every time she got frustrated for him (and with him, and about him) in his condition, now that it had a name, she stuffed the anger down with guilt and cried in the shower. That wasn't processing grief, it was silencing it. "What was I supposed to do? Have a funeral for our future? We have no idea how much time we have before he loses mobility, until he loses speech or the ability to use the bathroom on his own. There's no time to grieve a trip to Italy that we hoped for twenty years from now' ..."

What She Needs ...

If you've ever sat with a friend and listened to her open up about the deep, dark, thumping grief that is often hidden, you may not have known what to say. Or do. Saying nothing, doing nothing, is ok. For the friend, the confidant, holding space for she who grieves is generous.

On the other side, for she who grieves and holds this inside, this space is yours. Thinking along the lines described above creates a dynamic that may not be serving you. It may be preventing grief from processing. We've seen (and experienced) it supplemented with resentments and decreased attachment. Followed by guilt. And more.

Change is hard. Grief forces us to change. Choices are limited by the changes. Limited, but not lost. Leaning into the reality of this change would likely better serve us.

So, what does grieving properly look like? Is there a best way to grieve?

For She Who Grieves ...

"My friend's brother died a sudden death, though his twin brother was there with him, when his heart stopped. My friend herself, had been with their father when he died. She asked me, "Have you ever been with someone as they die? Witnessed the process? Their last breath?" I had not. "It is a privilege," she said, placing her hands over her heart, "a true honor."

This kind of thinking, about the honor and privilege of witnessing or experiencing such a significant process or moment, is a way of essentially embracing death; greasing the skids of grief, generating a more positive power, a momentum in a desired direction. Not to mention, when this friend was relaying funny stories that were shared at her brother's service, she was practically glowing, eyes watering from laughter. She clearly left that service feeling closer to people she didn't even know that well. Sad and sentimental over the loss of a loved one, but certainly more happy and hopeful than resentful.

We can accept that grief is inevitable. Unavoidable, really. We have a responsibility to ourselves to go through this experience. Truth is, there's no "right" or "wrong" way to grieve. It may not feel like it, but we do have options for how we deal with it, process, progress, and make it better. Do we honor it? Accept it? Deny it? Embrace it? Feel it? Heal it?

We believe that there is a biological need for humans to process the grief we feel. Not all people will experience grief about the same sorts of experiences in the same way. The sadness/grief line is drawn at different places. Some people move forward from a significant loss without grieving. As you'll see in our research for this book, we've learned that our grief response can be influenced in different degrees by our health, relationship and attachment style, age, education, race, gender, previous experience with grief, cultural background, belief system, knowledge around the loss, and even our financial and employment situation (Milic, et al., 2017).

You've likely heard of the five (or seven) stages of grief. And, reality check: none of them are easy. As we researched grief, we found many variations on the number of stages and how they are labeled, one even going up to 12! Even Elisabeth Kubler-Ross, who famously developed the five stages of grief in her 1969 book, *On Death and Dying*, expanded them to seven, decades later! In reality, some people won't appear to go through the stages of grief at all. And they may still be grieving in a healthy way!

Those who experience any of the traditional stages of grief may feel less alone when they learn their feelings are common. People who don't go through the stages of grief, however, may feel alone or stigmatized. Gross. They may even feel pressured to manifest outward signs of internal grief stages they do not actually feel. Double gross. The last thing anyone needs to be feeling while grieving is the pressure to grieve more.

While grief models are often used to help individuals who are grieving understand the process and how to move forward, not everyone experiences the same order of grief stages or even experiences every stage. We found it interesting that Kübler-Ross herself never intended for the stages to be a rigid framework that applies to everyone at all times. In fact, in the course of her last book before her own death in 2004, she said of the five stages of grief,

> They were never meant to help tuck messy emotions into neat packages. They are responses to loss that many people have, but there is not a typical response to loss, as there is no typical loss. Our grieving is as individual as our lives. (Kessler, et al., 2022)

Take that.

If you can imagine it, which we bet you can, the stages of grief are more rollercoaster-like than elevator-esque. The initial woopty-doos and downward swoops are a helluva ride at first, and ideally, there's eventually a lessening in intensity and duration, with the trusty clickity clack clickity clack it takes to work through a loss and journey up the next hill. We may still rush into an unexpected dip and experience a strong sense of grief, even years later, especially at certain events or special occasions.

That all said, given this is a book about grief, we feel we would be remiss in not describing the stages most commonly labeled. Simply being aware of potential grief "stages" and how you uniquely experience them can increase self-understanding and compassion. It can help you better understand your needs and prioritize getting them met.

Experiencing grief and working through the roller coaster of stages may feel S t R a N g E—all sorts of feelings might present themselves, including the feeling that you're going crazy (you're probably not), feeling like you're in a bad dream (wake up), or questioning your religious or spiritual beliefs (sit tight).

What it is	What it sounds like	What it may feel like
Shock—an initial response; can last for a few moments or many days; can reappear	"What just happened?!" "I just can't believe it." "Nooo!" "What. The. F*ck."	Trouble processing, emotional numbness, waves of incredulity...

It can also sound like nothing—completely speechless. There are no words. Shock can look like disbelief, and consciously—or unconsciously—resisting reality, for example, expecting the person or pet to show up, even though you know that's not possible. This gets into denial.

What it is	What it sounds like	What it may feel like
Denial—feels similar to shock, often experienced simultaneously	"This can't be real." "I'm fine/it's fine." "It's just not possible."	Confusion, avoidance, procrastination, difficulty focusing ...

This might look like staying busy. Or shutting down. Or even continually forgetting things. As negative as denial sounds, it's actually helpful for moderating our grief. Naturally, we can only take so much!

What it is	What it sounds like	What it may feel like
Anger—at yourself, anyone, everyone, and everything—it's also a natural emotion!	"This doesn't make sense." "Why?!" "What's the point?!" "This is absolute bullshit."	Rage, frustration, impatience, abandonment, resentment, need to blame ...

Pain is underneath our anger, and it demands to be expressed. It's completely reasonable to be pissed at (many) points in this shitty experience. The concern is in how you manage it. Being hurtful, aggressive or passive-aggressive, or having that extra glass, gets one into trouble.

What it is	What it sounds like	What it may feel like
Bargaining—negotiating our way out of pain	"I could've/should've ..." "If only ..." "What if ..."	Ruminating, guilt, shame, worrying, desperation ...

We so badly want things to return to normal. We will do anything to not feel the pain. "Please make it go away." Interestingly, in this kind of rejection mode, judging yourself or others and fear of being judged can creep in, as well as assuming the worst and even trying too hard.

What it is	What it sounds like	What it may feel like
Depression—a persistent sense of feeling down in response to significant loss	"It's too overwhelming." "Who cares?" "It's so unfair." "Why bother?" "Ugh."	Gooey sadness, emptiness, despair, disappointment, helpless, hopelessness...

A natural and appropriate response—for crying out loud, loss is depressing. This can look like crying, of course, or brain fog, sluggishness, reduced motivation and interest, or sleep and appetite changes. Depression can be a healthy stage of grieving, but people can get stuck there.

If you find yourself stuck in the muck of depression, it might be that early traumas or preceding losses are compounding it, or perhaps unresolved grief from the past is prolonging it. If old beliefs associated with depression or trauma surface, please, please seek the help you need to combat lingering hopelessness. We share some tips in this book to help dissolve the super-glue, but getting stuck here for an excessively long time can be really ruinous, so be kind to yourself, and obtain psychological assistance so your grief can evolve.

What it is	What it sounds like	What it may feel like
Testing—finding strategies to manage/rebuild/rebound	"Today was hard, tomorrow can be better." "I'll try that."	Wanting support, regaining control, hope!

Things start taking a turn! Yay! This can look like educating oneself, considering new perspectives, trying different strategies, being open to ideas. It looks like reading this book!

What it is	What it sounds like	What it may feel like
Acceptance—leaning in to (vs. resisting) the new reality; happens with/over time	"This has been a difficult experience, but I'm ok." "This is how it is now."	Courage, validation, self-advocacy and assertion, wisdom, hope ...

While denial looks like mindless behaviors or defensiveness, acceptance can look more like engaging with reality, learning to live with life as it is now. It looks like being present and self-compassionate, adapting.

Generally, when we are resisting acceptance, we are avoiding reality, say by sleeping more or using technology or alcohol or drugs to escape or unconsciously disconnect from our truth. We might stay focused on tasks, responsibilities, or the needs of others—staying busy as much as possible to avoid feeling whatever it is we don't want to feel or deal with. Sound familiar?

Acceptance sounds more like recognizing: "I'm ruminating on what I should have done or said; it's time to take that learning forward." You might acknowledge your anger and consider what it's really about, and/or self-validate: "Why wouldn't I be angry about that? Who wouldn't be upset about it? Of course it's hard to accept." Maybe it looks like self-compassion: "If I keep neglecting my own needs and focusing on work/others, or self-sabotaging with habits I don't feel great about, I'm destined for burn out. I'll take time to recognize how I'm doing and assess what I need. Now, who might I ask for help?" We can attest that there is some relief in acceptance.

We have more about acceptance later in this book; what's important here is that this is where we hope and want all of us to get to, to be!

In the 2020 drama series *The Wilds*, some of the characters are dealing with traumatic deaths, each in their own way (Streicher, S., 2020). One, of her dad and the other, a twin sister. How they experienced the "help" offered is played out for us:

Teenager Dot to Rachel: "I had a counselor give me a pamphlet on the five stages of grief. Dumb. Really dumb. There is no way that there's only five. You lose someone, and every new second feels like a brand new circle of hell. So I'm thinking, however many seconds in your lifetime that they're gone. That's how many. Just a billion little bullshit stages. So I'm not going to rush you. It's not up to me how much time you need. I just hope you're cool with company. 'Cause I'm not letting you stay here alone. So you got any good games we can play? Y'know, to pass the time a little?"

Rachel to Dot: "I'm not moving on. There's no leveling out of this feeling. I'm just ... I'm just tired. And as nice as you're being, I don't want you to watch over me like that. That was always her gig. And I'm just not ready to fill that position."

No matter how wonderfully written the pamphlet is (or the book, hmmm), the "billion little bullshit stages" take their sweet time and a wild ride working their way into the space where grief resides.

Spoiler Alert: What She Needs Is Different For Everyone

"Factors such as a person's social environment, how supported they feel, and the nature of the loss may also change how a person grieves" (Blandin & Pepin, 2016). To be honest, everything factors in– the stress level of one's job, the personal satisfaction a person experiences with their life or relationships, even the friendliness of their neighborhood! Studies have found a person's grief may depend on the loss. No shit. What we are interested in goes beyond the studies. It goes into the core of a person as they grieve, when they grieve, where they grieve, and how they grieve.

A 2016 study (Blandin & Pepin, 2016), for example, argues that people caring for a loved one with dementia face a unique grieving process. This is because they "lose" the person before they die but then experience another loss at death (more on grieving the living in the next chapter, we promise). The study proposes a dementia-specific model of grieving and argues that ambiguity is a core component of each stage of dementia grief. We touch on these concepts of anticipatory, ambiguous, and ambivalent grief too, in this book, as they have been experienced by our contributors.

One study found the most prevalent grief-related emotion was yearning for a lost loved one (Yale, 2007). Many people look for “closure” after a loss. David Kessler, who worked with Elisabeth Kubler Ross, proposes in his book, *Finding Meaning: The Sixth Stage of Grief*, that finding meaning *beyond* the stages of grief that most of us are familiar with can transform grief into a more hopeful experience (Kessler, 2019). He suggests that it can be more peaceful too, but the jury is still out on that, based on our interviews.

Grief conjures up so many mixed emotions—sometimes the accompanying feelings of guilt and shame can run throughout the course of grief, particularly when it comes to what was or wasn’t said, the things a person did or didn’t do. In some experiences, the feeling of relief when a person dies after a long, difficult illness, for example, may stir up some guilt as well. As women, the list of things we tell ourselves that we should be feeling guilty about has no end. So, let’s leave it there.

We recognize that there may also be a touch of shame in bearing grief in this moment, as it is being experienced now in the present place and time. This is a brave space. This is a safe space. This is a space for she who grieves.

What’s most important to take away from this moment is that there is no wrong or right way to grieve. People cycle through grief in their own way, at their own pace. Sometimes quickly, sometimes again and again in the same cycle, sometimes in a phase or a feeling for a really long time then back to another. Processing grief is not a one-time thing, nor is it sequential or balanced. Grief, like much of life, is messy, and perhaps one tends to experience certain elements or emotions but not necessarily in a clean or "correct" order or timeline or the set, same pattern for everyone.

Remember that roller coaster analogy? There are highs and lows. It is normal to experience ups and downs in mood, thoughts, attitudes and behaviors. "Cultural norms, personal factors, social support, health, religious and social values, and myriad other factors may affect how a person experiences grief" (Villines, 2019).

The 5, 7, 12, or 365 stages of grief provide a structure for better understanding, not an essential or step-by-step guide to success. If you don't identify with a stage, or note the overlap between stages, don't let it divert you from what it is designed to facilitate—awareness of your needs, so you can get them met.

We're not gonna sugar coat it: it's not all rainbows and fairy dust. Unicorn poop is still poop. It can be difficult experiencing any of it, let alone maintaining acceptance while things feel so unacceptable. Not to mention, many of us associate mess with stress and dread clean up. But listen, let's face it: we've overcome challenges before. And we know both mess and clean up can be satisfying! You can do this! We are here to help.

Trying to define grief, and make it something that is easily packaged up, is impossible. Author Jamie Anderson offers this:

> Grief, I've learned, is really just love. It's all the love you want to give but cannot give. The more you loved someone, the more you grieve. All of that unspent love gathers up in the corners of your eyes and in that part of your chest that gets empty and hollow feeling. The happiness of love turns to sadness when unspent. Grief is just love with no place to go. (2014)

Think it Out

Do women silence themselves to avoid discomfort when it comes to grief?

Is it self-preservation, or fear of being misunderstood, or just exhaustion?

What if we were taught that emotional pain is not "bad," just "real." And you need to feel to heal. Would there be less pain? More love?

Feel the Hope

Just for today, do one brave thing.

Create a space for yourself to feel something new, experience something new, become something new. Rock climbing may be a little extreme, but dig deep and look for one opportunity to be brave. Sometimes, the bravest thing is giving grief a name.

~*~

Giving Grief a Name

Like the highly respected, romanticized, and downright dirty work of paleontologists who study fossils to detect, classify, and name the scattered and buried remains of past life on earth; detecting, classifying, and naming grief can unearth evidence of past hopes that existed and a path to healing. In researching grief and how it evolves, we found ourselves questioning and hypothesizing ...

How much diversion away from the standard stages is still considered healthy?

Is it possible, or even healthy, to not grieve at all?

Digging in deeper to uncover the answers starts way back. What we think grief should be like starts to form at an early age by factors previously mentioned like spiritual beliefs, cultural attitudes, family history and social norms (Is it Possible, 2020). One of the biggest influences of what many people think that grief should look like is how it is depicted in TV and movies ... because we all know just how accurately real life is portrayed, right?

Let's get dusty and dig in a little more to the thought that there's no right or wrong way to grieve, and consider what happens to/with people who, for whatever reason, cannot/don't grieve (beyond not having permission). Are there people for example, who have been through complex trauma, or have emotional dysregulation, or various personality disorders, who are not able to feel, experience, or process grief? What happens to them? Are they any better or worse off? We can't answer that question. Not exactly.

In grief, there are different degrees of processing and different levels of functioning. Many of us may think we have processed our grief, and many of us haven't, but believe ourselves to be, or truly are, operating in life "just fine." Is ignorance bliss? Just like unresolved trauma that finds its way out eventually in some form or fashion, does unprocessed grief have a way of showing up elsewhere in disguise? Stories herein support our "yes" theory, but we haven't exact proof.

Some might feel underwhelmed after a loss, feel shame around not grieving like we would anticipate or feel expected to, and wonder why they aren't feeling more intensely about it. Is it normal? For the most part, our research says "yes" (phew!).

Are you seeing a theme here? We don't have all the answers. Nobody does. (Even paleontologists don't have all the answers about the creatures that stomped the earth eons before we were born!) We do know that just because something does not feel quite how we believed it would doesn't mean that there is something wrong or defective with us.

We aren't scientists, but we did find some reasons why someone might not be feeling grief as one would expect.

- Shock—When the loss seems like it can't even be real, it's no wonder you don't feel. You may feel like you're in a dream.

- Distraction—Focusing on the practicalities of the loss can prevent us from having the time to really stop and think and feel anything about what happened. You have lots to do and plan after a major loss. You're on autopilot, and the need to meet others' basic needs and the busyness of the times often gets in the way of grief.
- Avoidance—This is normal too, but when avoidance tactics replace coping skills, you may end up with bigger issues. Like if you refuse to talk about the loss (keeping in mind it's ok to NOT feel like talking about the loss sometimes), or continually deny the impact of the loss, or focus all your energy on taking care of others at the expense of yourself. Substance abuse is common in trying to avoid or forget the loss. And that just gets us a whole heap of other issues.

There's something called "absent grief," where a person shows no, or just a few, signs of distress about the loss of a loved one. Dr. George Bonnano is an assistant professor of psychology and education at Columbia University, with a Ph.D. from Yale University. He speaks about why some people don't grieve:

> There are clear outcome patterns, but they vary with different people. There are generally three outcome patterns: chronic grief, common grief, and resilience or absent grief. Chronic grief is someone who has a dramatic, high level of depression and grief after a loss, and they don't get better for several years. The common grief pattern is usually people who show an elevation of symptoms—depression, distress, difficulty concentrating, etc., and somewhere within

> a year or two, they return to normal. And the third type are those who don't show any disruption in their normal functioning. And that last pattern is very common. (Bonnano, 2021)

"Bereavement" is the period of grief and mourning following a loss. In some cases of bereavement, when someone doesn't show grief symptoms at all, it doesn't mean they didn't feel sad or miss the person, it's just that they were able to maintain relatively regular functioning. (Note, not much has been studied on resilience yet, though we do investigate it in this book!)

However, absent grief can also be a pattern of complicated grief considered to be an impaired response that results from either denial or avoidance of the loss's emotional realities.

Avoiding the truth and not allowing yourself to work through the emotions associated with grief can have negative consequences for your health if it becomes your coping mechanism.

Have you ever noticed that a toothache can only be ignored for a week or two before it demands attention? You might attempt to delay a visit to the dentist, but dental problems start small and often grow bigger. Grief can be like that too. "Delayed grief" can be a lot like a toothache. At one moment, you feel something awkward or even painful. Time goes by. Then, one good bite into a juicy apple and all hell breaks loose in your entire head.

The delayed onset of grief following the severing of a connection with someone else through a death, divorce, or other separating experience may not be recognized immediately but will come on strong at some point. Typically, delayed grief is brought on by another big event or loss—like another death, or the loss of a job, or just sitting at a green light when you really expected it to stay red longer. Delayed grief is also often caused by a difficult grieving situation, and when the dam breaks, it breaks.

Our attempts to process change and protect ourselves can get interrupted or sidetracked while we adapt to a new reality. Again, life is messy. That's reality. Even messier if persistent or complex trauma or traumatic grief is part of our reality, causing us to cycle (sometimes quickly and/or repeatedly) through the stages of grief, or remain stuck indefinitely. (We talk more about complicated grief and trauma later in this book.)

If one is grieving, and the grief is denied, numbed, or stuffed down, as with any negative emotion, we have found it will find its impact in and through us in other ways—likely negatively affecting one's health and relationships in ways that are less fulfilling than if we truly accepted, felt, and healed with time.

We believe grief can be ameliorated in healthy ways, and exacerbated in not-so-healthy ways. People who can't process or remain stuck in grief often suffer in insidious ways. Over the long term, they may or may not realize that their issues with relationships, addictions, and maintaining jobs, are a direct result of unprocessed emotion bound up in their limbic system and psyche.

The nature of grief can be difficult, and finding the right help can be too. We offer some resources in boxes throughout the book and at the end. Sometimes you just need to start somewhere, and ask to be directed to another possibility. A good place to start might be https://www.mygriefangels.org/

Yep, It's Complicated

As we've mentioned, grief is complicated. In our research, not only did we find there are nuances among definitions and stage models and effects, but we also found that there are a number of types, and many labels are used interchangeably and also vary depending on sources. Ironically, "complicated" grief is one of the many types of grief labeled. Often there is more than one term for the same description of grief, like "normal," "conventional" or "uncomplicated," or "typical" or "common" grief, and there are types of grief that fall outside the expected symptoms and reactions.

Some types, terms, or labels have to do with the nature of the loss (like "disenfranchised" and "anticipatory" grief), while others have to do with the response to the loss. For example, "typical" grief symptoms gradually fade over time; those of "complicated" grief linger or get worse. We are not attempting to present a comprehensive or complete list or glossary of grief. Everyone's grief deserves mention. We include concepts here that our contributors identified with the most. Again, labels can be helpful for understanding, but take care not to dismiss your grief if you can't categorize it, and please don't tuck your unique grief into too small a box, if any at all.

Complicated grief, also known as "prolonged grief," is when pain of a loss doesn't ease up over time, remains unresolved or keeps you from resuming your daily life and relationships. It's like chronic mourning (Smelser, et al., 2001). Complicated grief usually arises from the death of a loved one, where you get stuck in a state of bereavement, unable to accept the reality of the loss and, as a result, are reluctant to make adaptations to life. The psychological distress is characterized by intense yearning for the absent loved one.

Complicated grief can stem from traumatic grief. We found some distinctions that may be helpful to share—the term *complicated grief* is now primarily used to describe the experience of losing a person to natural causes, while *traumatic grief* is a relatively new term that combines trauma with bereavement or grief responses. For many people, any loss of a loved one is experienced as trauma, so we'll leave that thought where it is. That said, a traumatic event is typically defined as an event that poses a specific threat of serious injury or death to oneself or others, and elicits feelings of intense fear, helplessness, or horror.

The good news (ha) is that not all grief from trauma is "traumatic grief." The term "traumatic grief" is reserved for the psychological reaction following a traumatic event and for grief following the loss of a person during such an event (Fink & Bifulco, 2007). When provoked by the death of a significant other, it includes symptoms similar to PTSD (post-traumatic stress disorder) but specifically focused on the lost person, including intrusive, distressing preoccupation with the deceased, hypervigilant scanning of the environment for cues of the deceased, the wish to be reunited with the deceased, separation anxiety features, futility about the future, difficulty acknowledging the death, shattered world view, and anger together with impaired social functioning.

Not a light subject, we know. We promise it's not all this heavy. But we do get more into traumatic grief in Chapter 5. In Chapter 9 we talk more about releasing trauma and being brave.

A Few More Unpleasant Experiences to Learn About

Some people may minimize the loss of a pet, a friendship, or a job as something that's not worth grieving over. They *absolutely* are worthy of grieving. One may feel stigmatized after suffering a miscarriage because they "weren't far enough along" or sharing about the loss of a loved one through suicide. Maybe your relationship to a deceased person is not recognized because some people consider it inappropriate. This all can make it more difficult to come to terms with loss and navigate the grieving process. Elevating our awareness of disenfranchised grief or "hidden grief," which can occur when one's loss cannot be openly mourned, is one significant takeaway from this book that we hope you consider. Finding ways to grieve with the mourning is powerful.

Not being able to mourn openly due to lack of validation is one thing, lack of closure is another. Either way, ambiguity in grief is confounded as hell. The global pandemic that started wreaking havoc in the spring of 2020 left many mourners in its wake. We know that with sudden deaths, like Covid-related deaths, often it is not possible for people to attend the funeral, and this can be difficult. It's difficult to begin to mourn a loved one if it feels surreal. People can feel as though they have lost the opportunity to begin the farewell process, which is a fundamental part of mourning. This can keep us stuck in denial.

With the pandemic, some people are grieving over what they lost and the experiences they didn't get to have. Deep feelings of disappointment can arise when revisiting missed opportunities that never arrived. What happens when what we planned for never comes? What happens when what we had built our hopes and dreams for shatters?

There can be a lack of closure when grieving someone who is still alive or missing, which can fall into the realm of ambiguous grief or anticipatory grief. Anticipatory grief is grief that is felt prior to the loss of someone you love, often due to a terminal illness or diagnosis, like dementia mentioned earlier, but it can be sparked by a variety of circumstances.

Like other forms of grief, anticipatory grief can involve a mix of confusing emotions, particularly anger. On the flipside, anticipatory grief can also provide the chance to prepare for the loss, resolve any unfinished business, or say goodbye. Some people refuse to allow themselves to grieve before their loss has occurred ... uh oh ... does this sound like delayed grief?

As previously noted, there is much overlap in the grief world—categories can be helpful, but don't let them limit your deeper thinking or experience. We get more into all of this, including ambivalence felt in grief, in the next chapters.

Bottom line, as painful as it is, we believe it's important and helpful for grief to be felt and experienced, as it is part of the human journey, and as humans, we're in it together. If you are feeling overwhelmed by grief, loss, trauma, you do not have to go through it alone. If you're thinking that this might be a good time to speak with a professional about your experience of grief, it probably is. Check the back section of this book for some resources, or contact your healthcare provider. We'll wait.

Fortunately, and perhaps unfortunately, "grief will never have a clear-cut path, nor will it ever follow a pattern, and no theory on grief can ever explain how you will feel" (Miles, 2017). As with most significant experiences, over time, reflection on the range of emotions we feel allows us to make sense of grief and loss, and may make it less daunting to step toward a place of hope.

Think it Out

Does your grief have a name?

Can you identify the phases of grief as you have experienced them? Which were the most poignant? Which were the most obvious to others?

What emotions are conjured up by the idea of processing grief and loss?

Have you ever had to grieve the living?

Feel the Hope

Stop for a favorite cup of something somewhere today. Your neighborhood coffee shop, smoothie source, or a friend's house nearby. When you stop, really stop, and enjoy the something: a cup of coffee, tea, juice, or simply water with lemon. Watch the people around you. Look in their eyes. Not in a creepy way. Just be open to connection or even conversation. Connect in silence. Stay present throughout the entire cup, and be where your feet are.

Chapter 3: Grieving the Living

A note to anyone who needs to hear it: "We don't 'get over' or 'move on' from our trauma. We are forced to make space for it. We carry it. We learn to live with it. And, sometimes, we thrive in spite of it."

~ Unknown

This might be one of those topics you either get or you don't. Welcome to the ambiguously ambivalent world of grief.

For She Who Grieves....

"With this specific type of grief, 'grieving the living,' I think of it as abandonment. I chose to abandon my relationship with my mother. I choose the word 'abandon,' thoughtfully due to its definition; it is an act or instance of leaving a person or thing permanently and completely.

"When I was around 16 or 17 years old, I reached my breaking point when my mother AGAIN threatened to kill herself. She would always pull out this emotional manipulation card, but that day I had enough; I finally

decided that grieving her alive was a choice I had to make. I mentally and emotionally had to kill her off. I know that sounds sick, uncaring, and cruel, but I had to do that because of the emotional and mental torture and abuse of what she was putting my brother and me through. At that point I told her, 'Just do it. Please... At least the grieving process has an end. Living with this every day is just torture.' That was the moment I started grieving her while she was still living.

"You probably need a little background to what led me to emotional shut down. When I was 12, my stepfather sexually abused me. I told my mother, and she confronted him; he did not deny it. When he left for work later in the week, my mother packed up all of our belongings, and we went to my aunt's house in another city. Later when he came home and saw our things were gone, he thought we went to one of their friends' houses. Cell phones did not exist at this time. When he arrived at the friend's house, the friend told him we were at my aunt's house. My mother called the friend's house, and he answered the phone. My mother told him that he needed help, and her father wanted to speak to him. She also told him if he were to get help they could try to work things out.

"My grandfather called him at the friend's house and told him, 'You better take care of this problem before I do.' After they hung up, my stepfather went into a vacant house and shot himself.

"From that point on, my mother blamed me for his death. She started treating me like I was the 'other woman' who

wrecked their marriage rather than the daughter who just experienced sexual abuse by her husband.

"My mom struggled with drug use of all types throughout her life. The drug use got progressively worse after my stepdad's suicide. She started treating me like I was her enemy and would wave the suicide emotional blackmail card in front of me in an attempt to hurt me like she was hurting.

"By the time I had reached 16, I was like, 'do it please, and put me out of my misery.' I could no longer take the abuse and torture."

Maybe your grief is fraught with ambiguity and ambivalence. Maybe the person who died was abusive or damaging, or your experience of the person is wholly different than that of others. Maybe there was a lack of contact before death. "Ambivalence can be understood as a state of tension that occurs when we have opposing beliefs, feelings or behaviors towards a person, object, experience, or situation" (Miles, 2016). A degree of ambivalence is normal and to be expected in the grieving process. But for some, it can be incredibly difficult and painful to grieve when you experience conflicting emotions for the person who has died.

Ambiguity is the quality of being open to more than one interpretation, or inexactness. Often, grief or loss is "ambiguous" when it comes without closure. For example, when a person goes missing or the body isn't recoverable. Ambiguity seeps in also when a loved one is physically present but isn't psychologically there. Addiction, dementia, Alzheimer's, traumatic brain injuries and mental illness are examples when someone we love might become someone we barely recognize; they treat people completely differently, do and say things they wouldn't have, and they aren't there for loved ones in ways they were before.

When you suffer a loss that you're unable to process, when you're left confused about what has happened or why it's happened, it can leave you in this perpetual state of confusion without you knowing whether to accept the loss, what to do with it, or what position it leaves you in as a result of it. It's difficult to move forward with grief when you can't even wrap your thoughts around what is happening.

Another complication of ambiguous grief is that many people don't recognize it as grief (Vasquez 2022). When those around us don't acknowledge our grief, or make us feel that we don't have permission to grieve this sort of loss, it can make you feel lonely and isolated (enter disenfranchised grief). It can be a hard type of grief to open up about because we know others may not acknowledge it.

The value realized in finding a space to share, discuss, and unravel ambivalence, ambiguity, and other feelings, where aspects of loss are open for debate and reflection, is one of the primary drivers for this book. Sharing stories and talking openly about your thoughts with someone or a group that is able to listen well can be especially helpful. Psychotherapy is another opportunity to look in depth at the conflicted feelings you may have surrounding the loss and can enable you to explore in more detail how you feel and gain perspective.

As She Grieves ...

"Though I decided to abandon my mother in my late teens, I realized in my 30s that I had only abandoned part of her. I hadn't completely abandoned her emotionally, after all I would still answer the random drama-filled call from her, but something happened that convinced me to go through the full grieving process. One day out of the blue, she called. Every time I took a call from her, it affected my personality and how I interacted with my family for days afterward. My husband would say, 'Every time you talk to her, we lose you. And it's not fair to the family. We have to clean up the mess afterward. It's not fair to us who invest our energy and love you and support you.'

"The next time my mother called, I said, 'If you can't call and ask me how my family and I are doing before you dump all of your bullshit on me, don't ever call me again.' I abandoned the whole relationship and that person altogether. That was the day I mentally, physically, and emotionally buried her. I never heard from her again. Ten years later, I got the call that she died."

What She Needs ...

"Identify the parts of the grief: You have to be consciously aware when moments arise and ask yourself: 'Am I missing the person or the role?' For me, it's usually not her, it's usually the role. She could be a mean human. Most hurt people are mean humans. I don't remember her ever being a nurturing mother. So when moments like Mother's Day roll around, I'm a grieving child missing a nurturing mother. I miss the idea of what a mother would be like in

my life at that moment. When I was really small, my mother was a less hurt woman. When I need validation that she did love me, I will pull out a photo of her looking at me like a mother should look at a daughter. Sometimes a photo is all you have as a reminder of what used to be to help with your current void."

It can be tricky navigating past and present perceptions of the person: how they once were, who they became and your relationship as it once was, and how it changed. Remembering that the present doesn't necessarily override the past, or even in some cases, the past doesn't override the present, can be a helpful perspective. Either way, the positive can be cherished. It's helpful also to remember that ambivalence is a natural part of the grieving process and that ambivalent thoughts or feelings you have don't take away from the positive qualities you remember about the person. It's ok to allow space for conflicting thoughts. Thoughts are only thoughts, and you are not a bad person simply for having them.

There may be unfinished conversations, unresolved feelings. People and relationships are incredibly complex, as are the concepts of grief and death. Even separating current realities can be a way to work with ambivalence and ambiguity in grief.

"I use a helpful emotional separation tactic. I had to become really good with compartmentalizing life's events. I had to learn early on that—when I saw my mom doing drugs or saying hateful things to me—I had to separate the drugs from the person. I thought no one knew what was going on behind closed doors. I was really good at

playing both worlds: the home life of chaos, drug use, and sexual abuse and school/friend life of being outgoing, fun, and a good human. Compartmentalizing became second nature to me. I can acknowledge reality—it's not that I'm not coping with it or stuffing it. It's more about: If you can't do anything about it, why dwell on it—move on. By definition, that's resolving an issue. I also learned that, if you can't physically do anything about a situation, pivot and move on with actions you can control."

In situations where things like addiction, dementia, mental disorders, or brain injury are involved, when we understand that the illness isn't the person, we can better address difficult feelings like anger, frustration, and blame.

"I was seeing a psychiatrist for sexual abuse. I would tell him how my mother used drugs and was treating me like I was her enemy. I would tell him about the hateful things she would say to me. He provided me with coping mechanisms because she was lashing out at me over my stepdad touching me. He told me my mom was doing drugs to numb her pain; he also said, 'The drugs strip away a person, so that is not your mother saying those mean things to you. Those are the drugs talking.' He explained, 'God made mothers to be nurturing,' and that a mother would never treat their kids horribly, but drugs don't care who they hurt. That allowed me to mentally remind myself that it wasn't my mother present; it was drugs present. The Bible says to honor thy mother and thy father. I'm not going to honor drugs. I can separate the two. That was how I was able to do that."

Despite fear of judgment or misunderstanding, acknowledging and expressing one's grief, rather than ignoring or avoiding the pain, proves to be helpful.

"Sit with the grief. Feel it. Name it. If you're angry at something, say, 'I'm angry because...'—state specifically why you're angry or sad, or 'I feel abandoned because... I never had a chance to say goodbye.' Acknowledge it; call it what it is. Time will play a part in it. Whether you're saying it out loud or not, have conversations with the grief. Whether you are speaking to the one who passed, or the universe, or going for a walk, speaking to the grief helps you."

Gaining a new perspective on the relationship can also be beneficial. Considering that change doesn't have to be bad, as well as accepting that it certainly isn't easy, is eye-opening.

"This is critical: Once I was finally able to understand that I don't have to respect and honor her call just because the Bible tells me so, it made all the difference. Just because someone gave birth to you, doesn't give them rights over you and how you feel. I grew up with a religious upbringing. I was taught to 'honor thy mother and father.' ALWAYS. No exception. I have a new perspective now. If they want honor, they have to earn it. Just because you're created by their egg and sperm doesn't mean they earned that role and right of honor and respect."

The ambiguity inherent in these kinds of situations benefits from perspective and understanding, so connecting with others who can relate, and finding supportive groups and individuals is key.

"I've been very blessed to have so many amazing women who stepped into the mother role throughout my life, who were there for me. So I acknowledge those women and what part they played, so they know they are appreciated. I consider myself very lucky. I didn't just have one mom, I had 10! How do I stay healthy now? I surround myself with people who challenge me and support me, get me to look at things differently to expand my mind and my heart."

At times, ambiguous loss can be confused with anticipatory grief, the grief experienced in anticipation of death or some other life-altering event. Ambiguous grief comes from a loss that is unclear or without closure, and anticipatory grief is what one may experience when expecting a loss or change. We talk about that next.

Whether your grief or loss is experienced as ambiguous, ambivalent, disenfranchised, delayed, traumatic, complicated, or all of them, none of them, or more, the experience is what it is: painful and confusing. Again, labels can be helpful when understanding, explaining, and relating to what you might be experiencing, as long as you keep in mind what's really important:

Your grief, or non-grief, is valid.

Think it Out

What relationships have you mourned the loss or separation of?

What have you learned from each of them?

Where are you growing, personally, in relationships with others?

How does creating boundaries protect your spirit and safety?

What boundaries may need to be created still?

Feel the Hope

Step into your cocoon. Create a space just for you, whether it be a steaming hot shower with the door closed and music on, or a quiet bath. Your space may be solitude in the car, on your patio, or on a bench in the park. In this space, just for you, allow yourself time for stillness and the ability to check in with yourself. Come out of it when you're ready, and take note of how you feel.

Chapter 4: The Too Long Goodbye

"We could be tempted to wish that all good friends might wait to die on the same day. Those who have no affection would bury the whole human race with dry eyes and light hearts, such men are unworthy to live. Our sensibility to friendship costs us much, but those who possess it would be ashamed to be without it—they would rather suffer than be devoid of feeling."

~ Francois Fenelon, Archbishop of Cambrai

"Don't you dare leave without saying goodbye to Nonny!" A common joke in some families is the time it takes to say goodbye after a shared meal or birthday celebration ... individually bidding adieu to each member of the extended family can take upwards of 30 minutes. Fast forward a year, and as Nonny slips away little by little with dementia, the long goodbye begins. The long goodbye, which becomes the longing for her red sauce, the sound of her voice, the jangle of her rosary beads, signifies more than the loss of a loved one, but perhaps the loss of the connection with the past and anchor for the family.

For others, filing the paperwork for separation is just the beginning of the dismantling of a marriage that was planned to last forever. Each piece of paper, every swipe of the pen, each sock, shirt, and pair of slacks packed contributes to the long goodbye that signifies the loss of more than a marriage, each signifies the loss of the ideal, the loss of security in some way, and the loss of a piece of history. How does one balance the act of saying goodbye, which is an important step in managing the natural and healthy feelings of grief, sorrow, and sense of loss, with the angst experienced in the too long goodbye that prolongs the discomfort? We aren't sure. There you have it. We aren't sure.

Is it really okay to grieve before someone dies? And when they do, when does a person get permission to move on? What does permission to be hopeful look like? Only you can answer these questions, but only for yourself. Answering these questions for someone else just isn't fair.

It's worth mentioning that some losses are not just the loss of a person, it's a loss of an entire ecosystem. Losing a job, you lose the coworkers and clients. Losing a significant other, there's the severing of a social circle, as people choose loyalties with one over the other...maybe his friends' wives are no longer going to be friends with you. Not all relationships stay intact when a loss is involved. Aspects of your identify as it relates to others, and to yourself, have been lost as you experience this life change.

It's no longer just the loss of just what that loss was. It's the whole web. And you step out in the world as a different person.

We acknowledge grief to be complicated. Complicated by history, circumstance, the unknown, and many other factors. Perhaps you've realized this too. In your own experience of grief, complicated as it is, perhaps you've noticed that it doesn't isolate and present as a single moment or single cause. It's possible to grieve multiple moments in multiple ways. Furthermore, grief can be next-door neighbors to joy. Grief, coupled with anger, or anxiety, or gratitude, creates an altogether new experience that must be felt.

Saying Goodbye

The withering away of the body. The slow descent of memories. The dulling eyes. Slowing speech. Gasping breaths. For anyone who has watched another human being trudge through the slow fade of long suffering, each of these moments and milestones mark an experience of preparation and anticipation for the finality of death that comes for each of us. Long suffering challenges the living in ways quite similar to the challenge to the dying. Except one party gets rest, and the other lives with the other side of it.

The other side is a mixed bag of emotions, dragged through the rest of their lives if not properly sorted and grieved. Long suffering challenges us to confront our own mortality, but also to categorically acknowledge the many persons who the dying leave behind. The many "persons" sometimes inhabit just one body—the person who is dying. But the "persons" change over time.

There is the sick or weak version of the immortal soul that is leaving the world as we know it. There is the youthful version. The loving version. The angry version. Then there are the unknowns that sometimes become known after their passing. In the very best cases, the confluence of these persons is known and the long walk home to the other side is peaceful. In more unfortunate cases, the unknowns make their way to the surface, and grief is challenged with practicalities and consequences not anticipated.

Long suffering challenges us, as death challenges us, to realize that this is one moment that no one can run from.

There exists a powerful space between living fully and dying finally that must be handled with care. The preparation is a particularly painful and purposeful time in the lives of all those present. Sometimes, the focus on the painful elements prevents individuals from fully experiencing and processing the purposeful components. One does not ever "get over" a loss. The efficacy comes from moving through the loss and into a new and different space. And different can be quite scary.

The natural process of aging takes the whole family unit on a journey through history and evolution, presenting apt time for learning traditions and periods of expectation. Death and dying can be quite significant. In watching a parent wither and fade slowly over time, the emotions ebb and flow, and preparation for the inevitable departure is something felt deeply, mingling sorrow, grief, and fondness. Sudden declines in health, or emergence of fractures in the family unit, on the other hand, trouble those left behind for decades. When there's no time to page through history and ask important questions and seek resolution, the human mind and heart fills in the blanks by any means necessary.

Grief is an interesting phenomenon that 100% of humans will experience throughout the course of their lifetime, and for many, more than once. If this is a shocking fact, consider the reflection we invited you to do at the end of Chapter 1 ... a child's first grief may be the loss of a beloved stuffed toy or the discovery about Santa. We don't judge another person's grief based on what we are experiencing, and we don't judge our own grief in comparison with the loss of another.

Similar to the physical act of breathing, grief is something that is compulsory. Medical advancements in respiratory care and widespread training in CPR (cardiopulmonary resuscitation) have provided an opportunity for many people to live a little longer, even after cardiac arrest occurs, or something is lodged in the old windpipe. Unfortunately for us, there is not yet a device created that will restart our hearts as grief breaks them. That's the work each of us must do for ourselves.

For She Who Grieves...

"My friend lost her father suddenly. One day he was vibrant and healthy. The next day he had been taken by a stroke. His body lingered for more than ten years. But his voice. His laugh. His independence. They were all gone. She missed out on moments when she longed to hear his voice—introducing him to her would be husband, and later, sons. She loved his laughter and couldn't quite remember exactly how it sounded.

"When she speaks of him, there's a softness in her tone that indicates how special he was to her. They'd been through a lot together, and she missed him genuinely, but confessed that she didn't feel there was anyone she could truly share that with. She had to remain strong for her mother, who was devastated and not equipped for the constant care and needs of this man who had, not long ago, handled everything for the whole family, for their entire lives.

"Over time, the season of hope for recovery gave way to the season of longing for release. 'How do you grieve someone who is sitting in front of you?' she asked no one in particular. She was still grieving, years after he had been buried, perhaps because she didn't have the space to grieve earlier."

The long goodbye, the grieving of the living as they prepare for death, is closely observed by hospice workers and death doulas, who emotionally and practically support a person's good death as a trained companion. The front row seating gives insight to the delicate family dynamics, the histories and tapestries coming together, and the fractures that will bust up another generation. What can we take away from this? The sitting part. What it's like to sit with those saying goodbye, the long way. An intimate conversation with an experienced hospice nurse gave us much wisdom about grief.

"Hospice is about positively supporting this phase of life."

When a patient and their loved ones have tried everything and determined that further treatment is no longer advisable or desirable, hospice becomes an option. Hospice combines pain relief management with emotional support when it is most needed. The services are designed in a manner to not have any out-of-pocket cost for the patient or their family. While requirements may vary, for example by state, situation, facility, or service, it is never too early and certainly worthwhile to investigate this critical option.

"Please do not put off until the very last minute involving hospice. Grief is involved for all from the beginning, and compassionate listeners are always beneficial. A family or person should not, and does not, have to go through this experience alone.

"Hospice is not a death sentence. It's not "giving up hope." It's not admitting failure. This interpretation encourages families to procrastinate this kind of care. Hospice offers an opportunity for a quality of life as one faces this situation. It's about giving people hope for a quality of life until the end.

"If there's one thing I've learned, it's that we all need connection, community, people."

Hospice can be a huge relief for the patient and the family caregivers. Trained and experienced people are part of a team that can provide much support. Hospice is attuned to providing human connection, with objectivity. We all may need connection, community, and people, but at the same time, being able to listen objectively is important. As a family member or close contact, if you are hooked into feeling so badly about or for the person or situation, it can be harder to be truly helpful. Each person has their own grief, and they need to have someone listen objectively.

"It's impossible for family members to be entirely objective because they are coping with their own grief. When caring for a person in hospice, your own emotions have to be kept out of it, so you're not over-identifying and projecting your own pain on them. It's about THEM, not about YOU. You can't listen helpfully to them if you've got your own imaginings and deeper connections going on."

Likewise, often the patient wants to protect their family members—they aren't always comfortable being honest about their own pain or thoughts with family. Patients often want to hide their own emotions from family—so hospice staff is there to listen.

"For the hospice staff, the opportunity to debrief with other staff is important for remaining objective—and practicing self-care—recognize what helps you take care of yourself and not dwell on what you know someone is dealing with. Staff supports each other. And not being overworked—pace yourself so you don't get swallowed up in it."

That's good advice for anyone caring for a grieving person.

Being seriously ill or having a frightening diagnosis can be a lonely time for all involved. When one is sick or grieving, people often do not know what to say.

"People have to be accepted and met where they are. When you're with a person who is sick and grieving, it's

important to stay present and focused, not be rushed. Whenever I found a place of common interest, it helped me make a connection with them. Attention spans are short, and fatigue often arises quickly, especially when visitors are involved."

So what do you do for someone who is sick? What do you say to someone who is grieving?

"Be a good listener. People don't want platitudes or phoniness. Make eye contact. Some people like to have their hands held; some people don't want touch. You have to be sensitive and read the person. Find out what they are interested in—sometimes you don't have to ask—you can just observe—like if you notice they have a Bible or poetry book on a table. Start a conversation. Phrases like, 'I understand why you would feel that way,' or, 'Tell me more,' can also be encouraging.

"Helping people do things other than feel sick is important. Finding something to connect over, like doing a puzzle together, is really helpful. Music also makes connections. It gives people something to talk about. And reading out loud—there is research that suggests there are benefits of reading aloud not just to children, but to the reader, and to older people in nursing homes, for example.

"When my aunt was in the nursing home, I used to sit with her and five or six other women, and they didn't really have a topic of conversation. But if I would bring in a book, a poetry book for example, and read aloud, people would recognize it or chime in. This brings joy."

Every person and every situation is unique. "*Let them lead you. It's so individual, as is each situation with families and relatives and unfinished business.*"

Unfinished business. That's tough. When people have a bad relationship with a family member for instance—hospice can help work through ambivalent feelings or encourage reconciliation in some way, even just helping them write a letter. Whatever a patient feels is "unfinished" is a reasonable favor to ask of hospice. Like putting together a photo album, writing a letter to family, reading aloud to the end of that good book. Especially when there is no family, hospice volunteers can do a lot to help a dying person tie up loose ends.

Another key tip from hospice (and a reminder for all of us any time): *"It's really important not to make promises you can't keep. Keep your word—don't break their trust with something like, 'I'll be back tomorrow,' then not show up."*

There is hope in trust. It's easy to forget that grieving people can still experience hope and joy, and so desperately want to. When the hope for recovery has been lost, there remains hope for the best experience possible. Hospice can be offered as a beneficial, positive way of supporting life until the end.

"There was a young woman at the hospice facility longer than usual, an art student, who started doing collages; she was attached to a portable morphine pump and was not confined to her bed, she could walk around as far as the cord would allow. Her friends had set up a table at a big window, and she busied herself with different colored

papers. I brought her wrapping paper for example, and friends hung her collages on the wall.

"I felt really good about it because she and I were connecting, and I was providing reinforcement for her creativity and an affirmation of her abilities, instead of focusing on the illness. I looked forward to going into her room. It was nice to have a conversation point, to discuss the art ... it was a point of creativity but also beauty ... a very positive experience to visit her."

Eventually the staff made it possible for her to have an art show of her creations in one of the hallways where families and others could admire them. Color. Joy.

She also recalled another experience. Where a woman's daughter brought her in, and left her in the hospice room. *"She had beautiful clothes on, pretty fabrics, and she was sitting in the chair, crying, when I came in; she had been left to change into an ugly plain nightie. 'Is there anything I can get for you?' I asked. 'I can't get in that bed!' She didn't want to get in this sterile white bed. I didn't blame her!"*

Colorful quilts, comfortable fabrics, on the bed or to go over shoulders, can really make a difference. *"Photos for the patients bring joy, pets can come in and out—that brings joy, too. Flowers bring joy, color—they need color in the rooms, not sterility."*

"My experience as a hospice nurse reinforced how important people are to each other. We all are to each other. How important it is to relate, and how little it takes.

It doesn't cost a lot. You don't have to bring big gifts. It's the companionship. The human connection."

In his book, *The Four Things That Matter Most* (2014), Dr. Ira Byock, an international leader in palliative care, talks about four simple phrases that carry enormous power to mend and nurture our relationships and inner lives:

"Please forgive me"

"I forgive you"

"Thank you"

"I love you"

Originally from a Hawaiian practice of reconciliation and forgiveness called Ho'oponopono, these four phrases and the sentiments of repentance, forgiveness, gratitude, and love they convey can help someone let go of life, as well as help us resolve interpersonal difficulties with the living. These affirming words can help us practice integrity and grace in our day-to-day lives, inspire harmony, and improve our emotional well-being.

According to Mary-Frances O'Connor, a psychologist who researches grief at the University of Arizona:

> Humans are predisposed to form loving bonds, and as soon as you do, your body is loaded and cocked for what happens when that person is gone. So all systems that functioned well now must

> accommodate that person's absence. (O'Connor, 2021)

For most people, the systems adjust. "Our bodies are amazingly resilient," she said.

Much has been written about the relationship between love and grief, and the agonizing pain of losing the object of one's love. According to medical doctors studying bereavement, one way to think about grieving a loved one, they said, is that the feeling of connection to the person who died "gradually moves from preoccupying the mind to residing comfortably in the heart." Preoccupation subsides, and that's good. We are not sure that the undercurrent of grief, or love, ever really does.

Saying Hello

Basic, reasonable relationship needs and expectations can be amplified during grieving and benefit from extra attention. Companionship and belonging, verbal and/or physical affection, emotional support, and validation can be so helpful when one is struggling. We all want to live our lives with a sense of acceptance and affiliation. We all want our hurt to be recognized and repaired.

When we are grieving, people taking an interest and expressing care through words, touch, or action, and being willing to help meet our special needs and find solutions together helps us feel accepted and respected and loved. When we are grieving, we need that most.

"Some of the best things said to me when I finally shared my pain, were simple things like, 'I'm so sorry that happened to you,' 'Thanks for sharing this with me,' and 'What would be helpful? What do you need?' It was like instant relief. I could feel myself relax deeply in that moment. Essentially the critical message there was, 'I believe you,' and 'I am here,' and that made all the difference."

Understanding the complexity of grief, may create a little space. Often, space is just what is needed to heal. Knowing yourself well enough to determine how much space you need, and when and how to reveal, share or withhold your experience of grief is not a science. It's a careful attention to the tolerance you have for uncomfortable situations and vulnerability in that moment. Have you revealed to yourself or someone else where you're at in your journey?

Every day presents each one of us with an opportunity to access, actualize or accessorize our grief. Will it be something that accompanies you into a conversation on your arm? Something unveiled to open a deeper connection? Something that brings out the colors of your true human self? Or shall it be layered upon or put back in the closet ... for now. You can choose when to use it as a tool to forge relationships and self-actualization, or not. You can acknowledge where you are in your grief on that day and make it accessible, or not. Did you have a crummy day? Maybe today you reject the session. Where are your feet today? Maybe you'll risk the leap. Will you claim it, aim it, or avoid it?

Picture this. You've just moved into a new neighborhood. You've been invited to a dinner party and you're planning to attend; after all, these are the people you'll be walking past in the mornings, and very soon, you'll learn their habits and interests. You spend a little time considering what to wear, what to bring, and how you'd like to introduce yourself. Casserole or bottle of wine? Summer dress or nice pants with heels?

It's been a while since you've been the new girl in town, and were you imagining it, or was there a hint of hesitation in that invitation you received from the oh-so-polite neighbor, Paulette, who just happened to also be the realtor who sold you this gem of a property. You're unsure of yourself these days and how people perceive you, but you feel the need to step out. You wonder what people wonder about you, in this new life. Are they making up their own stories? Should you set them straight?

Let's introduce you to a few characters you will be dining alongside this evening.

Norm lives in a nice three-bedroom home on a typical suburban street, actually on the cul-de-sac, and drives an unassuming four-door sedan. Norm is well known by these neighbors, respected by his community, and is quite congenial if you happen across him on the sidewalk. Norm is that steady eddy neighbor, who, you have noticed, is starting to gray a bit at the temples. He's aging, but then again, everyone does.

Ann is one sharp cookie. She's seldom late, in fact, she arrives before the dinner party has started and fixes herself a cup of coffee right at the kitchen counter. You know, precisely where the food is being prepared. Ann is a great listener, intense, and has the ability to get under your skin by pointing out something that you weren't quite prepared to acknowledge. Ann's not at all unbearable, but you do get a bit nervous around her from time to time. Once she shows up, it's hard not to think about things. She can be a good friend, or a frustrating adversary.

DeeDee can be the life of the party, but she's always late. It's hard to pin DeeDee down for an event, and if she says she'll be there, you can guarantee that the party will have started before she makes her grand entrance. Funny enough, rumor has it she's come in full costume a few times, and it wasn't even Halloween.

Cate always has a concern. Cate has a few doctors on speed dial and doesn't always want to talk about what's plaguing her. She doesn't say much, but you sense that it would be good if she had someone who she could open up to.

~*~

Paulette is there, the natural hostess. And now that you're here, surrounded by this cast of characters, and a few others who faded into the background more or less, you're confronted with something–The moment when they ask you how you ended up in this neighborhood, on this block, in this house. Alone.

You weren't always alone. You had someone. SOMEONE. And friends. And hosted dinners like this. Until you didn't.

Until the loneliness became all that was left because THEY left. The people from your old life, your old you, your old easy-as-it-goes. The grief of going from being someone TO someone, with a life full of someones ... to alone. It's an awkward sort of grief ...

Yes, this is your moment to share your grief, and spit out the words that burn in the back of your throat every day. When you wake up in the morning. When you walk to the kitchen. When you pick up your keys. When you lay your head down at night ... alone.

You recognize that this group is comfortable with each other. They know the habits. Cate is gnawing at her fingernails at this point, and DeeDee spits it out again, "How'd you get here? You single, honey?" As you open your mouth to say those well-rehearsed words, you notice Norm. Looking awkward and at ease all at once.

Quickly, you lay your grief out onto the table for everyone to see, hear, dissect. You squeeze your eyes shut tight, and suck in a slow breath. Then—Silence.

Norm gets another scoop of whatever smells so darn good. DeeDee changes the subject, now to *her* dating life as she pours another glass of wine. DeeDee didn't know alone like you did. It was easy for her to breeze through the muck and find something new to focus on. But Ann stares at you, directly in the eyes, and nods knowingly. Had she been *alone* before? Did she know that grief?

Cate begins to fixate on the details of her dessert fork and then starts asking questions better directed toward her own medical professional. Cate is complicated, and it seems like everything somehow just got a little trickier with her health situation.

People respond in the way they're wired, and it's awkward. This shit is awkward.

The experience of grief, at a dinner party, for example, can be surprising. While everyone grieves differently, everyone reacts to the presence of grief differently. If we know everyone grieves, in their own way, then why does it feel awkward at times to experience our own or someone else's grief? Can't we just accept that everyone grieves something or someone at some point and find comfort in that unfortunate fact?

It's awkward to be in a community where they have an expectation of you to be normal, yet you've lived through this experience which makes you unlike them in other ways. However, on some level, you know it's likely everyone has something like that, some regrettable recipe, some burnt torte. On the surface it doesn't look like it and it doesn't feel like it, but it's likely at some point, they've asked the same question: What if they don't want me because what I'm serving up isn't as tasty as the apple pie or as potable as the chianti?

When you're carrying grief, it's a strange experience to be around a group of people with whom you want to forge relationships or a connection. Nobody wants every first hello to be a therapy session. It can take some time to recognize where we're at and understand the dynamics of a situation.

Whether we choose to bare and share our grief, risk our vulnerability, depends on the quality of our relationships, our ability to trust, our wisdom whether or not to trust, trust in our own judgment, and fear of others' judgment, invalidation, or disbelief. Our level of security in our own feelings, and in the situation—are we defending? Sharing? Bonding? What's the purpose of the share? Are we responding to someone else's grief or prompting a reaction, a desire to be seen? Do we just want to be understood, be accepted, and feel a sense of affiliation? It might depend on what we're grieving, if guilt or shame or embarrassment are involved. It may depend on knowing the benefits to sharing or having experienced regrets in having done that.

And each day, you are going to walk in a room, you're going to have an opportunity to assess, access, actualize, or accessorize your grief. It can be what it is, what you want it to be. You'll know your tolerance in that moment. You can choose to expose a piece of yourself to being respected, supported, and loved; you can try on radical vulnerability; or you can decide it's not a good time. You can allow yourself to be in a cozy cocoon, or give a TED talk. There's empowerment in knowing it's your choice.

Turns out, Norm's wife of 25 years and mom of two teens died quickly last year of a rare, aggressive breast cancer. Ann cared for her mom with Alzheimer's for years and, as a medical professional and Ph.D., felt she should've been able to save her. DeeDee was completely duped by a con artist, was left at the altar, and made the decision to never commit to anything again. Cate had a rare disease at an early age that stole her childhood.

Does grief become another thread to pull people together? Yes, if you allow it.

We have our everyday lives. Then we have our heart-lives, which we shield fiercely. Saving the heart-lives matters. It's the relationships that matter. Somebody has to hold spaces for people to be brave ... to share ... to live hope ... even if it's simply in line at Chuck E. Cheese ...

Think it Out

How do you navigate the detachment for self-preservation without severing the close relationship with the dying?

How do you talk about your grief?

How do you react to learning about the grief carried with those around you?

Where does your support come from?

You have suffered a loss. You feel changed. How do you reveal this new identity to people?

How do you determine if it is safe? Is it comfortable? Is it going to separate us or bring us closer together?

Feel the Hope

Initiate a check in with someone who you care about. Make it count. Ask someone what you can do for them today. Ask the questions that reveal the tender points, and respond honestly as you are invited to speak. Your responses may be different, having been working in your grief. Make the moment with the living greater in value by fully tuning in, and when you say goodbye, rest easier.

Chapter 5: Trauma & Grief (and the Brain)

"Trauma is the response to a deeply distressing or disturbing event that overwhelms an individual's ability to cope, causes feelings of helplessness, diminishes their sense of self and their ability to feel a full range of emotions and experiences."

~Unknown

Everyone experiences trauma differently. Much of what is shared in this chapter is based on support, education, and personal counseling received by contributors via a combination of many area resources. For more information, or to seek help, please call your local crisis center, or use the resources found on the last page of this book.

For She Who Grieves...

"After months of therapy with an esteemed therapist, I asked, 'So what the hell happened to me?!' As soon as she summed it up in a small but powerful handful of words, my reaction was a cynical retort, 'Well that's rather dramatic.' She was clearly frustrated and called me out.

'Why do you push back every time you ask for objectivity? I give it to you, based on decades of experience with this kind of thing, and you negate it.'

"I was speechless. It was true. I asked for objectivity because I was so confused as to my experience, and even years later, none of it felt so bluntly black and white as that. It just wasn't in my realm of imagination, so it took so very long to accept the truth. The day she said that, several years into my 'recovery,' was the day I realized, once I broke it down word by word ... Holy shit. She's right.

"That was when my recovery took a turn.

"Yet it still wasn't fully cemented. One day a friend was listening to me have a panic attack over being sued by my former partner, hyperactively ranting about how it was bringing up horrible memories of feeling violated and powerless. Noting my behavior, he said, 'Have you ever talked with this local crisis agency? It's affordable, and they really helped me with PTSD.' Even then I negated, though not as firmly, 'Would they really accept me?' It's not like I was ever held at gunpoint, roughed up, or beaten.

"This was the same friend that early on in my trauma journey, as he had experienced his own trauma, thought it might be a good exercise for me to privately write down everything that I had experienced, line by line. Get the specific pieces out of my head and on paper. Even after I did that—this was years prior to the therapist mentioned earlier—I tentatively asked him, upon reading him my

list, 'What happened to me?' And he looked at me very carefully and kindly and told me what he thought. I didn't accept it then either.

"Believe it or not, I had denied it even prior to that, when lightly describing a piece to a dear friend in another state, who quietly gasped in tender horror. I rolled right over it, explaining the behavior away, even though I was calling her from the house I had escaped to.

"My first night at the agency was eye-opening. Sitting around the table, learning about PTSD and realizing: 'Holy shit. I belong here.' So much of it was making sense."

"Trauma is an emotional response to a terrible event like an accident, rape, or natural disaster. Immediately after the event, shock and denial are typical. Longer term reactions include unpredictable emotions, flashbacks, strained relationships, and even physical symptoms like headaches or nausea." (*Trauma*, 2008)

Just like grief, trauma and its effects are subjective to YOU; everyone experiences this a little differently. Similar to healing and to grief, it can look a little different for everyone. And oh, yeah, PTSD is not just something that veterans experience.

Some people experience PTSD and/or grief with trauma, while others don't. PTSD looks a bit different than grief, although certainly there is overlap. People who suffer from PTSD often relive the experience through nightmares, flashbacks, difficulty sleeping, avoidance, detachment, emotional dysregulation, and anxiety attacks seemingly out of nowhere. Sometimes, the trauma sticks around and doesn't go away on its own. Sometimes, the trauma needs a name. A plan. A place to live until things start to get better.

There are many resources to help people work through the after-effects of traumatic experiences, and we mention several in this book. Much of the following can be attributed to the experience and the personal notes from one of the brave women who shared their stories:

- PTSD can occur in anyone after experiencing or witnessing life-threatening events. It can also occur after experiencing physical or sexual abuse as a child or adult.
- PTSD associated with interpersonal trauma is often overlooked.
- Risk factors associated with PTSD include early adverse life experiences, lack of social support following trauma, previous history of trauma, and if it's interpersonal trauma (e.g., betrayal, loss of a relationship/person).
- PTSD can interfere with daily living and can interrupt the healing process. Symptoms can last for a short period of time, months, or even years; they can begin right after the event or surface months or even years later.

With complex PTSD (stemming from chronic, long-term exposure to trauma in which the person cannot foresee a time it might end), in addition to those symptoms, there is a change in self-concept—how one sees themselves, their perpetrator, their morals and values, their faith in others or a god. Symptoms and how they present vary and can be as unique as our biology.

When a person is experiencing trauma and PTSD, especially complex PTSD, there may be more confusion around processing grief. We know that while its specific effects are subjective, from a biological perspective, when trauma is experienced, what's true for anyone is that their overall emotional function is impacted to some degree.

A Brief Brain Class[1]

A brief explanation of the parts of the brain and how it works can be helpful for also understanding grief, especially if you are curious nerds like us. While we certainly aren't neuroanatomists, there is agreement among the scientific community about how the brain develops and that trauma can impact the brain and its development at any time. Picture us with a pointer stick at a chalkboard diagram in the front of the class, please ...

---

[1] Information about the brain is adapted from PAAR distributed material on "Trauma and the Brain," which references these resources:

Resick, P.A., Monson, C.M., & Chard, K.M. (2017). *Cognitive Processing Therapy for PTSD: A Comprehensive Manual*. New York: Guildford Press.

Van der Kolk, B.A. (2014). *The Body keeps the Score: Brain, Mind and Body in the Healing of Trauma*. New York: Viking.

There's the brainstem, the limbic area, and the prefrontal cortex.

- **The brainstem,** often referred to as the "primitive brain" or "reptilian brain," begins developing *in utero* and regulates the involuntary and instinctual responses like reflexes, muscle control, breathing, heartbeat and balance.
- **The limbic area**, or "emotional brain," is the middle part of the brain that perceives, categorizes, checks for danger, and experiences emotions. This is where the thalamus receives messages through your senses and decides where the information should go next.
- **The amygdala** is the fear center deep inside the brain; this area is outside of our conscious awareness or control and is where the question, "Is this a threat?" is answered. When the amygdala is activated we feel afraid, shocked, reactive, and/or vigilant–this generates the fight, flight, or freeze response. (We are aware of the variations of the "F" responses but are sticking with these traditional three for simplicity.)
- The **hippocampus** receives the information next. This is the "memory filing cabinet" of your brain. It runs new information by previously stored memories and experiences for similarities.

Stick with us here ... it all comes together eventually ...

- **The prefrontal cortex,** known as the "thinking brain," is located behind your forehead, near the top of your head. It's responsible for the abilities and qualities that make humans unique from other mammals. Rational thought, speech, sense of time, problem solving, personality, planning, empathy, and awareness of ourselves and others happen here. *When this area of the brain has been strengthened, we are able to think clearly, be confident in our decisions, and be aware of ourselves and others.*

- Located next to the prefrontal cortex, but deeper inside the brain, is the **anterior cingulate cortex (ACC)**. This area is responsible for regulating emotion closely with the prefrontal cortex. *When the ACC has been strengthened, we are able to manage difficult thoughts and emotions without being completely overwhelmed.* This area helps us manage our emotions so we don't do things we regret.

Now bear with us, this is where it gets good, honest.

When the brain's alarm system is turned on, we go into "survival mode" and automatically experience preset physiological responses in the brainstem and limbic area, particularly involving the ACC, amygdala (fight/flight/freeze), and hippocampus. It can take the prefrontal cortex a little while to catch up. Science has shown that over time, this can change with cognitive and body-based therapy techniques.

There are two important parts of your nervous system that play an important role in our body's physiological responses to events; in turn, these physiological responses have an impact on the functions your brain is prepared to perform.

- **The parasympathetic nervous system** is responsible for the "rest and digest" response. This allows the body to repair itself and restore it to balance. Heart rate and breathing is slower, muscles more relaxed. The parasympathetic response helps improve digestion, conserve energy, and maintain overall health.
- **The sympathetic nervous system** controls the "fight or flight" response. Another common response is the "freeze" response: the complete inability to respond or immobilization.

When the "warning signal" system in the brain is activated, the hippocampus (the "memory filing cabinet") changes from encoding and consolidating memories to pumping cortisol (stress hormone) in the body to prepare for a physical challenge or escape/retreat. This hormone activates targeted muscles and organs, ensuring you are active and alert so you can survive. Your heart rate increases, breathing is faster, muscles contract.

What you might not know, Smartypants, is that traumatized brains look different from non-traumatized brains in three predictable ways:

1. The prefrontal cortex/rational or thinking brain is UNDER-activated.
2. The ACC/emotion regulation center is UNDER-activated.
3. The amygdala/fear center is OVER-activated.

Here's the most important part: With the more primitive limbic and brainstem areas highly activated, like a hyperactive amygdala, and the cortical areas of the brain under-activated, we experience chronic stress, vigilance, fear, and irritation and can't think clearly.

- A traumatized person may have a hard time concentrating, feeling safe, calming down, or sleeping.
- Survivors of trauma can experience difficulty managing emotions. A simple scare for example, may bring on a rapid heart rate long after the joke is up, or impede "letting go" of minor annoyances. With an under-activated ACC (emotion regulation center), even when you want to calm down and feel better, you just can't.
- What you also might not know is that there are often no words to attach to traumatic experiences because traumatic experiences are encoded in the brain differently. Remember that the center for speech production is in the prefrontal cortex. When the amygdala senses danger, the brain stops the processing progression and prepares for fight-flight-freeze, before it even gets to the hippocampus or prefrontal cortex. Your brain also releases extra amounts of natural pain relief, vasopressin and norepinephrine, which provide strength and slight amnesia.

Because of this and the hippocampus switching from encoding and storing memories to pumping cortisol, processing of stress—or trauma-related memories—is rerouted. *They are not in the place in the brain where you'd usually find them.*

- As a result, it is difficult to consciously access these memories. Unlike everyday memories where there is typically a beginning, middle, and end, with traumatic memories, the story may be incomplete or have no sense of time or order attached.
- Traumatic memories may be fragmented, with missing pieces. Unlike traumatic memories, everyday memories tend to be easily verbalized and emotions associated with remembering are not overwhelming.

Bottom line: Traumatic experiences impact the flow of processing information in the brain. *For our bodies to heal* (e.g., from post-trauma responses like constant exhaustion, muscle pain, dizziness, or headaches), *we need to be in a parasympathetic (rest and digest) healing state.* Healing releases the intensity. And, as you will see, healing is possible!

Ok so here's what's REALLY important—you can change your brain! Yes, it takes effort and time. Time well spent and effort so worth it. A specialist in trauma and PTSD who uses evidence-based methods that change the brain by working with both the body and the mind can help you make these changes. See our chapter on Releasing Trauma and Being Brave, specifically.

For She Who Grieves...

"I was being intentionally violated in many deep and personal ways, essentially as punishment for becoming emotionally involved with an old friend, despite knowing better, and fearing even mentioning it to my then partner. For a long time after the worst of the discovery and ensuing hell was over, I have grieved the near total loss of my psyche, safety, and sanity during that disturbing and troubling time."

As She Grieves ...

"Enough damage was done that year and for quite some time afterward that, for a decade, I have been in therapy for post-traumatic stress disorder symptoms and have taken antidepressants and anti-anxiety meds. It took me a long time to realize what I had actually experienced."

What She Needs...

"I didn't dare tell anyone for a very long time. The last time I shared my truth, my story, I lost two solid pounds, no joke. Literally, it's like a weight was lifted. With various types of therapy for PTSD, like eye movement desensitization and reprocessing and energy work, my hyper-vigilance and hyper-sensitivity have finally mellowed, I am triggered less readily, and I know how to address my triggers in the moment. Even my crying spells that would occur suddenly out of nowhere have diminished."

"Sometimes viewing the traumatic event objectively in your mind with the guidance of a professional can help. Like becoming the objective observer, say, from across the

street. You won't get rid of the memory; it's about getting a different emotional response. When you view it as the event itself without the emotional intensity, it becomes more empowering, or less disempowering, and changes what the meaning of the memory is to you."

"*When you are feeling triggered, Ground yourself. A technique is to look above eye level and notice three things you see, two things you hear, one smell, one taste. Squeeze your finger. Pick something up and notice it tactilely. Literally feel your feet on the ground. Even better with your shoes off!!"*

Please see the Releasing Trauma and Being Brave chapter and the rest of this book for a deeper dive into what our contributors have found helpful in finding relief.

Just as what one person grieves, another one might not; what traumatizes one might not traumatize another. That doesn't make either person's reaction or response wrong. Just like if someone else is not grieving something that you are, it doesn't necessarily mean they're numb, dumb, in denial, or limited in their abilities to feel or accept. What might be traumatizing to you and how you respond to trauma might not be the same for someone else. There are various stages of trauma and healing that might overlap with, but aren't necessarily the same as, the way grief stages are typically outlined. Not only is the cause individual, the process can be too.

It's important to note here, given that grief and the specific effects of trauma are individualized, that healing is too. A realization of ours that might seem obvious but bears repeating: Different things work for different people at different stages and at different times. We talk about this next.

Think it Out

Are you capable of identifying signs of trauma in yourself?

Do you take the effects of trauma in your own life seriously?

Are you healing the causes and effects of trauma and grief, or treating the symptoms?

What has been helpful to you in your most difficult moments?

Feel the Hope

Sit or stand before a mirror, and speak out loud to yourself those four things we offered: "Please forgive me" – "I forgive you" – "Thank you" – "I love you." Allow those kind and tender words to yourself to say what has not been said in the way that you have needed it before. Surrender to the moment. It's okay to feel. You are okay.

Chapter 6: What's Next?

You don't just lose someone once,
you lose them over and over,
sometimes many times a day
When the loss, momentarily forgotten,
creeps up, and attacks you from behind,
fresh waves of grief as the realization hits home,
they are gone........again.
You don't just lose someone once
You lose them every time you open your eyes to a new dawn,
and as you awaken, so does your memory,
so does the jolting bolt of lightning that rips into your heart,
they are gone.........again.
Losing someone is a journey, not a one-off.
There is no end to the loss; there is only a learned skill
on how to stay afloat when it washes over.
Be kind to those who are sailing this stormy sea; they have a journey ahead
and a daily shock to the system each time they realize,

they are gone .....again.

You don't just lose someone once, you lose them every day,

for a lifetime.

~ Unknown

~*~

In the midst of loss, mustering up the guts to be open to the next moment, the next day, the next page, the next year, and eventually, the next hope, sometimes feels insurmountable. For she who grieves, hope is waiting for an invitation to accompany her into the next.

Maybe you're asking yourself the following questions:

What do I do now?

What is the help that I need?

What's a step I can take?

We believe that deep pain, grief, and trauma that aren't dealt with appropriately find inappropriate ways out and blur the way to healing and resilience. There comes a time when you need help. Especially with a complex crisis, to peace out, it can help to piece it out, and view your overall situation like spokes of a wheel.

Sometimes many of us are dealing with overwhelming amounts of pain from multiple situations simultaneously, and we have to approach the journey to healing one spoke of the wheel at a time. In a crisis state, you might have to put out the fires in your mind one by one; then eventually tease out what is chronic, what you haven't dealt with yet. Baby steps! Or toddler steps if you prefer.

As we've mentioned, how you grieve and heal depends on many factors, including your personality and coping style, your life experience, your faith, and how significant the loss was to you.

Inevitably, the grieving process takes time. It's an organic recuperative process. Healing happens gradually; it can't be forced or hurried—and there is no "normal" timetable for grieving. Some people start to feel better in weeks or months. For others, the grieving process is measured in years. Whatever your grief experience, it's important to be patient with yourself and allow the process to naturally unfold (Smith, et al., 2018).

While you're letting the process unfold, there are various strategies to help you gain control in optimizing your physical functioning, psychological issues, and relationships with yourself and others. Supplement the healing process with practices that have compounding benefits. Remember, different things work for different people at different times.

We include here the opportunities that the women we spoke with found to move forward *as she grieves.*

As She Grieves ...

"I didn't even realize it until several years later after I left that partner, that on some level, with unavoidable

ongoing exposure to them, I have been grieving a slow, subtle chipping away of my soul. Even though it has been a constant energy drain to manage the mind-fuck and soul-suck of twisted abuse, and a battle to protect and maintain my own personal power, I am coming out strong."

What She Needs ...

Acknowledgement. Acknowledging very consciously how you feel is a good first step. Verbalize the feeling, and then practice letting it go. Statements like the ones below are often used with an alternative treatment called "emotional freedom technique," often referred to as "EFT" or "tapping" or "psychological acupressure," and can be used whether you are aware of what that is about or not!

"Even though I'm feeling ____, I'm open to letting it go."

"Even though this feeling is so deep and I can't imagine letting it go, I'm open to that possibility."

"Even though I'm experiencing ____, there is an opportunity to ..."

"Even though I believe ____, I choose to ..."

"Even though I've thought ____ for so long, I'm willing to think ..."

"Even though I am not totally comfortable with ____ I choose to respect this discomfort ..."

You can help the grief along by acknowledging and validating it and guide it in a healthy direction. Identify the feeling. Speak to it. Of course you can always speak to someone else, too!

"Through albeit limited sharing of my experience, I have received confirmation of the surreal reality I experienced and validation of the resulting grief and struggles I've endured. It was a completely crazy-making time, and I have needed assurance that my experience was real, and my fear and grief were valid. Objectivity and validation of one's experience are especially important with psychological trauma."

As She Grieves ...

"I do recall one dear confidante early on who threw me off. She was trying to be understanding and logical, yet it felt like she was minimizing, even justifying and rationalizing, my partner's behavior, almost playing devil's advocate. I think she was just trying to be fair, since without hard "proof," (and clever deception on the partner's part) everything seemed questionable. Or maybe she was rationalizing and justifying some of her own private behavior. Regardless, it was not helpful. I felt misunderstood, invalidated, and even more unsure of my reality."

What She Needs ...

Validation. **And empathy**. Talk with someone who listens to understand and can acknowledge that your thoughts/feelings/circumstances are valid to YOU—

possibly for reasons they DON'T understand. For clarification: empathy is not sympathy. Empathy isn't about agreeing or condoning. And just because you don't necessarily share a person's concern, doesn't mean it's any less valid. Even if there are similarities in experience, everyone's experience is unique.

"I've shared my experience with a few wonderful therapists, eventually certain trusted friends, and limited family members. Their response, thank goodness, was validation, compassion, and care.

"Through my experience, when listening to a grieving person, I have learned not to minimize or dismiss their grief in an attempt to empathize of make them feel better, with comments like, 'It's not so bad ...,' 'Look at it this way ...,' or 'Couldn't you...?' Please don't play devil's advocate. A person's experience with grief is their own, to be dealt with on their own timetable. People need validation of their deep sorrow. Sometimes just listening and saying, 'Wow, that's a lot,' or 'I don't know what to say,' is enough. Also, please know that just because your own experience with grief may be different, it doesn't make yours or anyone's wrong or any less real."

How we are responded to when we undergo trauma makes a difference. What do we need to accept in our own grief? In someone else's? That it's valid. However we or they are experiencing it. It is their own reality. Their truth at that time. It does not make sense to judge or dismiss something that is true to someone else, that is someone else's own experience that you cannot possibly fully understand. More on judgment in the Sharing the Ugly chapter.

Even if your experience is different, it doesn't make yours or anyone's wrong or any less real. It's so important to recognize that just because you don't share someone's view, it doesn't mean they are wrong—it just means you think or feel differently.

What does this kind of validation do for us and others? It meets our basic human need to feel heard, valued, respected, supported, trusted. It also helps to validate one's OWN experience. Try, "*Even though I have this event in my life, I choose to be OK.*"

As She Grieves ...

"I have always been introspective, but I learned new things about myself, the impact of my own past, how prior events have affected me and made me vulnerable to certain things. What that means, how to be aware, accept, move with discoveries in a way that brings out the best me."

What She Needs ...

You may have heard a lot about the term "acceptance." Acceptance doesn't mean not experiencing distress, emotions, or trauma. Accepting your loss doesn't mean agreeing with what happened, and it isn't the same as forgetting it either. Your memory of what or who you lost is an important part of you, and over time these memories can shape and define who you are. Acceptance is not resignation. Just like empathy is not condoning and resilience is not resistance. They aren't negative concepts; they are positive.

Acceptance is more about realizing "it is what it is," from a factual standpoint, it's a shift in focus from something we don't have control over to change, to something we can. It's a way of moving forward. Acceptance means noticing what you are fighting against, validating your desire to fight against it, and re-orienting yourself to the reality of the moment you are in. In terms of the previously mentioned "Acceptance" stage of grief, it means not getting stuck, or getting un-stuck, from other stages. Mindfulness and a non-judgmental, curious attitude can be a big help when it comes to acceptance and understanding.

"Acceptance is not settling. It's recognizing where you are without judgment, and then getting curious about your next options." ~ Merilee Smith

As She Grieves ...

"I wish I had learned sooner that I was trying to heal an emotional experience mostly intellectually, and that can only go so far."

What She Needs ...

Understanding yourself and your situation are both important. "You can't grow if you don't know" has been said by many in the educational arena. Educating yourself is always a good thing. Clarity around what might be happening and why, as well as what our options are, can be helpful in making better choices and finding the right solutions. Hence the content of this book.

“Your pain is the breaking of the shell that encloses your understanding.” ~ Khalil Gibran

However, this is an important point: Please accept that the “why” isn't always going to get us where we need to be, and spinning wheels trying to figure out something elusive may not unlock the freedom being sought. Accept what the situation is, as it is now. “Emotional sobriety,” a term coined in the 12-step community, is when you accept that you can’t understand “why” in a way that makes sense. Not everything is logical or rational, or even determinable. It’s also about being comfortably present with your feelings and being able to process distress—beneficial to anyone in any community.

As She Grieves ...

“Sometimes I have had to put the grief on a shelf and tuck it away. And it slips out, like when I’m putting one of my children to bed and thinking of the ones who aren’t there. Or when July rolls around and my body demands that the marking of my birth, which was accompanied by the last miscarriage, is remembrance of something else. I hear that as years go by, this will be less intense. I hope so. I’ve recognized that if I don’t soak up the grief when it hits, it will soak in and come back in another wave.”

What She Needs ...

Being present. The present is tomorrow’s yesterday and yesterday’s future! Say what?! We’re just saying that today matters, this moment matters. Usually when you’re angry or sad, you’re thinking about the past or the future. So bring yourself back to the present. Dealing with what is in the now, as painful as it might be, aids acknowledgement, acceptance, and validation; eases processing; prevents ruminating; and allows us the space to grieve and feel, to heal, and even to experience joy.

"You have all the knowledge you need. Stand in quietness to hear it." ~ Unknown

By the way, meditation or mindfulness to support being present doesn't have to be an extensive process of focused attention. Try starting with breathing while stating an affirmation that feels good to you (see further below). Or simply try this: *"I connect to the force that guides me, flows through me, and makes me stronger."*

Balance "being in the moment" with positive thinking to guide your next steps.

As She Grieves ...

"It's pretty rare that I give up hope. Nothing that I was trying was working. I've been resilient in life. When it was just me, before having children, I had the freedom to just move to the next thing if something didn't work. I've always been able to make a different choice. I've been able to go in a different direction, get to a different place. The first time that I experienced that hopelessness—it was primordial pain. I couldn't fix this thing. Where was my magic now? It was gone, and I couldn't change this. I didn't know if that was grief, but it was there. Since then, the grief has been more subtle. Maybe for the past several years, I've been stuck in some phase of grief and didn't

realize how much it was holding me back from living my best life. I often felt like I was going two steps forward and one step back ... or one step forward and two steps back. I couldn't get a break."

What She Needs ...

Recognizing where you are, and where you are trying to get to, and where you might be stuck can support acknowledgment and acceptance and emotional sobriety.

For getting unstuck, try asking yourself, *"If I make the decision (to leave, to release the guilt or pain, to live well, whatever), will it get me to a better place/space/way of being? What areas of my life would be most positively affected?"* Also consider what you are getting from NOT making the decision you are debating. What is procrastinating doing for you? What is the alternative behavior doing for you? Does it make sense that it is outweighing the benefit of making the decision? Is your prevention of joy based in fear? Consider what it is costing you to NOT make that decision. Then make the decision! Again, baby steps. Commit to baby steps. It doesn't have to be perfect. You can always make a new decision, choose a new direction.

"But he was able to understand one thing: making a decision was only the beginning of things. When someone makes a decision, he is really diving into a strong current that will carry him to places he had never dreamed of when he first made the decision." ~ Paulo Coelho, *The Alchemist* (1988)

Bob Proctor (rest his soul), another well-known speaker in the personal transformation field, shares very practical information about what making a decision can do for you and how overcoming excuses and "buts" can lead to happiness and contentment. "Making a decision" with Bob Proctor is worth a Google.

Take time to evaluate your situation, and try imagining the optimal.

Try This—Pick up your cell phone, and make a voice recording for yourself. Read the following statements slowly so you can close your eyes and fully experience this visualization activity. We are inviting you to privately and securely visualize yourself in the future in possession of what you desire or in a desired state. Put on your inner weirdo hat if you need to. First, record the prompts; then, hit play to hear your own voice speaking back to you, and close your eyes ...

~*~

Record ...

I will visualize my future—a future that is full of hope.

I am quiet now and listening.

I am finding myself in a space that is free from distractions.

I am finding myself in a space that is safe and secure.

As I engage all of my senses, I look around.

I look up.

I look around.

I look at my hands and everything within my reach to touch.

I look down at my feet and notice where my feet are planted.

I look around, again, noticing this time, the space that I am occupying and all that my eyes can see.

I look up, take a breath in, and release it slowly.

Who am I with?

What do I touch?

What distractions are starting to come through, if any?

What can I do with them now? Put them aside, or allow them to take up space and just be?

What are the feelings that have begun to stir?

What brings me joy?

What would an ideal day be in this reality?

What do I care about?

What do I want to manifest?

What choices can I make in that direction?

End Recording

~*~

Since you just recorded yourself, hit play, and listen to your own voice. Pause the recording to answer the questions for yourself.

Taking the time to be with yourself and speak to the peace and calm that is needed for healing and hoping is not something that is often prioritized. Perhaps this has been the first time that an experience like this has been presented. If this was helpful and productive, revisit it. If it was not, move on, and try something else.

"Do what makes you happy, and you will be healed. Quit what dims you. Bring the world your gifts." ~ Unknown (though likely Wayne Dyer or Alan Cohen)

As She Grieves ...

"I would wake up each morning and say, before my feet hit the ground, 'I can do this.' It was a mantra I learned from a friend in a similar situation. I can't tell you how those four simple words boosted my spirit for the rest of the day."

What She Needs ...

Affirmations are helpful for getting into appreciation mode, setting the right vibration. (I choose to ... I am ... I can ... are good sentence starters):

"I choose to experience my grief in a new way."

"I am not alone in grief."

"I am allowing myself to ..."

"I can be comfortable with ..."

"I am clearing any doubts around ..."

There is something to be said for practicing thoughts of happiness, appreciation, and hopefulness. It is said, "Where the focus goes, the energy flows." It's okay to be anxious or disappointed. Just don't stay there too long because it holds you off from who/how you want to be.

Maybe what you see as negative is actually opening up room for something positive.

As She Grieves ...

"Eventually I came to a place of self-compassion. Understanding. Acceptance. Thoughts like, 'What's done is done,' and 'This too shall pass,' have been helpful mantras. Taking deep breaths. Appreciating miracles. Knowing that the inner wisdom of our body and our mind is helping us without us necessarily even being aware. Gratitude."

What She Needs ...

Like affirmations, **gratitude** is founded in positive energy. Emotions are energy. You may have heard the quote by author Neale Donald Walsch: "Emotion is energy in motion" (1995). A revelation of 21st century science is that all emotions trigger biological reactions that shape your health just as distinctively as what you choose to eat or how you choose to exercise.

> When you learn to change your emotional reaction to a situation, you change your biological reaction as

> well. How you react emotionally is a choice in any situation and these choices can make or break your chances for well-being. (Orloff, 2010)

When you come from a place of fulfillment and abundance, you create a positive effect. A scarcity mindset makes you play small. Play bigger! Try "I'm grateful for this life and the magic I get to experience in it," or simply list three things you are grateful for each day for 21 days.

"Happiness is letting go of what you think your life is SUPPOSED to look like and celebrating it for everything that it IS." ~ Mandy Hale

As She Grieves ...

"My friend mentioned my journaling. I scoffed and said, 'I don't journal. I haven't written in a diary in years.' She just about spit out her beer. 'YOU don't JOURNAL?! You have about 5,000 post-it notes around your house with thoughts on them. You have handwritten affirmations stuck to your mirror. You text yourself your views on relationship issues. You have saved receipts with ideas scratched on the back. That's journaling!' I had never thought of it that way."

What She Needs ...

Journaling has been referenced by our contributors as a great way to process grief. You don't need to be a "writer." Even just noting what you're grateful for and listing some affirmations counts. It can also serve as a memory support when your thinking is fragmented, helping you understand

and recognize your situation, and giving you perspective that leads to acceptance.

"You should see my stack of notes and articles and books and notebooks. Not only is it an outlet, and even helpful to return to for perspective, but I love the look and feel of paper. I love the feeling of pen connecting with paper. It's like being barefoot and connecting to the earth. Innate satisfaction."

"I was so grateful for my listing-of-exactly-what-happened exercise years later, because when I go back to look at that list now, I can see objectively the overall reality of the details that were fresher at the time."

As She Grieves ...

"I discovered a new kind of self-love and respect, by identifying my values and beliefs and what I will and won't accept, how to set boundaries, and what to do if someone continually violates them. What to say. What it truly means to compromise, when to bend and when not. Loving yourself more than others isn't selfish in a bad way; it's fundamental."

What She Needs ...

Self-care can't be emphasized enough. Sleep, exercise, and diet are so important for grieving healthily and setting yourself up for success. These aspects of self-care all have significant impacts on our mental stress.

Affirmation, gratitude, and journaling practices are part of self-care, too; this is the spoke of the wheel that for many of us, is the LAST spoke to be replaced, if at all. Why? Why don't more of us prioritize our self-care? Of course we know that if we get mentally or physically sick or die, all hell will break loose. We dread having our own failure or underachievement in any area being the cause of anyone else's grief.

We grasp the airline's logic of putting on your own oxygen mask before helping others. On some level, we know that self-care is important. We don't seem to recognize or accept HOW important it is on a deeper level. We don't prioritize DOING it. We challenge you to commit to the necessity of it. Discipline!

Self-care and self-compassion are part of loving ourselves in healing. So often we are hard on ourselves, for feeling a certain way or doing/not doing something. There's nothing wrong with wanting to control our emotions, improve, do our best, be responsible, and have a high quality orientation. But why do we do that at the expense of our own physical and mental health? We tend to our partners, friends, and children—what about nurturing our very own precious souls?

"Selfish" is only a bad word if it is at the true detriment of anyone else. We are so conditioned to believe that if it isn't for somebody else, there's no value to it, which creates the belief that our own internal desires are second. When, in reality, doesn't the quality of what we give come from greater personal fulfillment? A fuller cup? (And we don't mean coffee, though that can help.) We've all heard of the inner critic, self-sabotage, and imposter syndrome. Ditch that drama, embrace yourself, and prioritize the process of your true health, renewal, and new growth! This includes caring for your soul. We're not kidding here folks.

Try this. Just be still. Feel your "soul seat" (near your heart and collarbone), put your fingertips there, or press your whole hand there, and ask, *What do you want me to know? What do you need from me right now?* Listen. Compassionately. Put aside any judgment of the "out there" nature of this. Breathe. You might be surprised of the instinctive insight and guidance provided to you.

We agree that, "intimate and loving relationships are the most powerful and enduring source of happiness." This quote came from Clayton M. Christensen, author of the business book first published in 1997, *The Innovator's Dilemma*. He commented on the propensity of people (we presume men, given the era) who are driven to excel to overinvest in their careers and underinvest in their families, and recommended investing time in the latter.

We venture to hypothesize that the propensity of women to underinvest in themselves and overinvest in their spouses and families, is directly affecting the quality of their intimate and loving relationships, let alone the essential relationship they have with themselves. And the time and space they are (not) giving themselves to grieve. The most powerful and enduring source of happiness, starts with our intimate and loving relationship with *ourselves*.

In our collaborations and research, we have learned that one of the most essential things you can do in addition to connecting with others, is connect with yourself. Try to focus on self-love and self-care and give back to yourself something to enjoy in the process of mourning. We put talking to someone you are comfortable with and trust in this self-care category. Releasing difficult feelings, disappointments, and pain out of your body, even through journaling, is all part of self-care.

"Learning what it means to 'love yourself' is what I have learned specifically through grief."

Bottom line: there are ways to come to terms with your grief, embrace it even, and eventually find a way to move ahead with your life. We believe key elements include acknowledgment and validation of your grief, understanding and acceptance of the facts, affirmation and gratitude for the positive pieces of your life, being present and recognizing the state you are in and wanting to get to, and support and self-care to get there.

Think it Out

What does radical acceptance of self look like for you?

What role does affirmation have in your healing journey?

What will hope bring to life as you know it?

Feel the Hope

This is your invitation to create hope for someone else. Make a donation of time, goods, or money to one of the organizations mentioned in this book or one that is close to your heart. It doesn't matter how much, it matters that you respond to the invitation to create hope. At the very least, know that hope can be found in a simple smile.

Authors' Note: Information shared in this book regarding finding relief is based on contributors' real experiences with seeing welcome improvement. The information provided is not intended to recommend any particular resource or diagnose, treat, cure, or prevent any disease, nor is it intended to be a substitute for professional medical advice. Always seek the advice of your physician or other qualified health provider with any questions you may have regarding a medical condition, mental health condition, or medications.

It is critical to seek professional attention if you think you are suffering from an anxiety disorder, depression, trauma, or prolonged grief. Many free and sliding-scale services exist in more places than you realize. Ask. Do not let finances deter or prevent you from seeking professional help.

Part 2

Chapter 7: The Best Was Yet To Come

what I'm learning about grief ...
is that it need not be
a heavy gray shawl
to wrap myself in,
clutching my arms tightly
across my chest

nor ...
need it be
a granite rock
that I should try
to push away

neither is it ...
... at least, no longer ...
a vast dark ocean
ready to pick me up

and slap me down
without warning

what I'm learning about grief ...
is that it is not me,
but that it offers
to become a friend

a friend ...
who will lightly lay a hand
on my shoulder
when tears come in the dark

a friend ...
who will laugh
out loud with me
at remembered silly moments

a friend ...
who can still hear
the music of our life

what I'm learning about grief ...

is that this friend
doesn't intend
to leave me

but promises
to hold my hand
to carry my memories

a friend ...
who will bear witness to my love
as a venture
toward the next day
and the following night
~Nancy Cross Dunham

~*~

If you are finding the dance between grief and hope to be filled with up-tempos and dramatic pauses, electrified by charges and struck by lightning, then this journey we've invited you on has been meaningful. When the worst day of your life has already happened, what is there to be afraid of?

We all know someone who experienced the worst day—the woman at home with her newborn who receives a call that her husband has suffered an aneurysm; the couple who puts their healthy baby to sleep and finds that he succumbed to SIDS in the morning; the family that goes on vacation and returns home to a fully flooded home; the person who cashes in her IRA to start her own business as the global pandemic shuts down commerce. These worst days happen. They can and do happen to anyone. What do we make of the after? How does the worst day become the first step in what will come next—the best, yet to be known.

This is where hope springs out of fear. This is where magic happens. This is where the honest appraisal of possibilities and needs meet. This isn't for everyone, and acknowledgment of that is not a judgment. Moving from the worst day of your life to hope might not happen like a bolt. But when it does, if it does, that's ok too. It doesn't make your experience of grief any less mournful. It doesn't make the loss mean any less. It means that your grief is serving a purpose that is going to change things for someone else. For she who grieves, the desire to press grief into service is significant.

If you look closely, you'll find women who have turned grief into hope.

For She Who Grieves...

"I woke up in the middle of the night with the same feeling as the night before: storms raging in my body, lightning and earthquakes jolting me awake. My heart was pounding, and millions of terrifying thoughts were racing through my mind. I felt panicked, like an atomic bomb had been dropped on our family ... We just wanted this scary night to be over, but we also knew that when it

ended and daylight came, we would be going to our daughter's viewing." (Sheykhet, 2020)

~*~

Pittsburgh, Pa.—October 8, 2017

A University of Pittsburgh student who had recently filed a protection from abuse order against her ex-boyfriend was found dead in her off-campus home. Alina Sheykhet, 20, was found Sunday morning by her father, who broke down her bedroom door after she failed to answer calls. Alina's parents experienced the most devastating event they could ever imagine. Elly and Yan, Alina's parents, express the grief of her violent murder as unbearable. However, they created hope. In the writing and publishing of the book, *One Year After: From Grief to Hope*, and promoting the passing of Alina's Law to protect victims of domestic violence, Elly champions hope. Elly provides evidence that pain and grief can coexist with hope, and even when it doesn't feel like it, survival is possible.

"After losing a child, you lose yourself. Life is now divided into two parts: the 'Before' and the 'After.' In this book, a bereaved mother unveils her road map for navigating her new world without her child. One Year After gives you a different understanding of life and death. It shows a connection between two worlds—a physical world and a spiritual world. When you are confronted with the intense suffering that comes with losing a child, you can live in the memories of love that you shared. The greatest power that we possess is the power of love. It gives us strength and forces us to continue living, even when we feel like dying."

In loving memory of Alina Sheykhet

1997–2017

~*~

Pittsburgh, Pa.—August 24, 2016

Grief can sometimes be cyclical. Our bodies recognize the time, the physical experience, the spiritual memorial, the mental exasperation, as much as our emotions do. When Katie Stern, mother of three, came into our lives, she had already experienced the unimaginable.

Katie's story, as originally shared by the Rhett Sullivan Foundation in 2019, is as tender today as it was then. We sense it will always be.

For She Who Grieves...

"August 24 was a normal morning—we got up and got Luke and Toby ready for the babysitters, and we got ready for our work day. I drove the boys to daycare, got Luke out of the car and carried Toby inside in his car seat. I kissed both boys and said "I love you both. Be good today. Dad will pick you up, and I will see you at home." That afternoon around 2 pm Toby went down for his afternoon nap, and he didn't wake up. Dan and I got the calls while we were at work, and Toby was transported to the hospital without us. Dan made it to the hospital before I did and watched as 20+ medical staff tried to revive Toby. When I got there, it was nearly 5 pm. Toby was pronounced dead at 4:12 pm. On my drive to the hospital

all I kept saying repeatedly was "Toby, I'm coming. God please help him." The next time I held Toby, he was already gone. We sat with him until 10 pm. Leaving him in the hospital room with people who didn't even know him was one of the hardest moments, of that time in our life, I ever experienced.

"We miss watching him grow; playing with his brothers; not hearing him laugh or take his first steps. We miss every moment of him not being here, down to the things that most people take for granted.

"In our grief, we started a foundation in Toby's memory in 2017, almost a year after he died. Dan and I knew that Toby's life and story had purpose and that his memory was meant to live on through us. Our foundation donates Owlet Smart Socks to families welcoming an infant to provide peace of mind for the parents and caregivers and monitor the infant while they sleep.

"Toby's death has changed my husband and I and Toby's older brother in many ways. Dan and I don't feel like we will ever be the same people as we were before August 24, 2016. Emotionally, many things still make my heart break—watching siblings together, hearing Luke talk about Toby and knowing how much he misses him, certain times of year—holidays or birthdays. Financially we were blessed to have the support of our family, friends, and community after Toby passed away."

Katie's grief became a force of hope for families—and at the entrance to the Inaugural Gala in 2021 was a hope-filled memorial for Toby and the other "Hall of Angels" babies who left this world as he did. Many of the parents and families who have lost their infants to SIDS were also present. Through the efforts of Katie and the supporters of The Little Fox—Toby's Foundation, they are able to fulfill donation requests for Owlet monitors, placing them in homes of families who have experienced a loss, families expecting multiples or pregnancy complications, or families that may not be able to afford an Owlet.

In loving memory of Tobias "Toby" Graham Stern
May 27, 2016–August 24, 2016

~*~

Pittsburgh—December 2018

Attending a wedding and a funeral for the same person in such a short period of time is unnatural. But for many of Lori and Matt Keener's friends and family, this became a reality. Lori and Matt were overjoyed to be the parents of their six-month-old son, Ryan, and had just left mass for some last-minute Christmas shopping. Matt had a sudden and unexpected catastrophic brain bleed and died on Christmas Eve. As impossible as it was to make sense of this, Lori found the courage to allow Matt's death to save the lives of many. Because Matt was young and healthy, his organs were ideal for creating Christmas miracles—six—that Christmas Eve. Although Matt and Lori had never talked about Matt's intention to share this gift, it was made possible in the raw moments of Lori's grief.

Lovingly and bravely, Matt's mother shared this idea with Lori, and Lori was open enough to say "yes." When the woman who brought Matt into the world and the woman who loved him so significantly, chose to share him as a gift, they created another significant connection that changed so many lives. The Center for Organ Recovery and Education (CORE) helped people who were waiting for years for a lung or a liver. CORE refers to organs being donated only as "gifts," and this vocabulary change was very meaningful to Lori and the rest of their family.

Being a gift was so much a part of the love that Lori and Matt shared, bringing Ryan into the world being the first, but not the last, visible demonstration of this. Had Lori's mother-in-law not looked at her, in all her grief, and offered a chance at building hope for another family, those six miracles may not have happened (Jantz, 2022).

In loving memory of Matt Keener 1975–2018

~*~

Turning grief into hope doesn't have to be a loud moment. Sometimes it's the quiet nod of acceptance for what has just happened and releasing the expectation that everything is going to be ok. Some things are not ok. And that's ok.

When things are absolutely not ok, hope can peek through the darkness. The hope-peeking-through takes many forms. For many, the hope-peeking-through is Tiffany Huff-Strothers.

Tiffany recognized her gift to uplift at a very early age, as her family became the billboard example for the epidemics plaguing the black community: drug abuse, single parenthood, gangs, poverty, and divorce. Nonetheless, Tiffany became the first in her family to graduate college and received numerous scholarships, including one from The Bill & Melinda Gates Foundation to attend graduate school. In the midst of her graduate studies, she found herself in a relationship she had no idea how to end, and seemingly suddenly went from hardworking mother and student to heartbroken and homeless after being shot by her first love.

In her book *30 Day Stay: One Woman's Story of Escaping Death, Healing from Heartbreak and Finding Hope in Homelessness*, Tiffany explains a different kind of grief and resilience, when she fell to rock bottom—homeless, heartbroken, and trying to find hope while healing from years of wounds that were now being exposed on the 11 o'clock news. *30 Day Stay* is a story about one woman, but it is also a story about any of us who find ourselves in situations that require us to move bravely through and around the grief of reality not being what we had hoped, mustering up the courage to reinvent ourselves from the ground up ... while everyone is watching.

Tiffany turned her grief into hope in a very public way, in 2011. She found that she and many of her family and friends were single mothers, in need of support and encouragement to get healthy. She started E.M.P.O.W.E.R.

(Encouraging Meaningful Progress Overcoming Weight Empowered by Results) a holistic health support group that generated a loss of more than 200 pounds in six months for the group! Simultaneously, the *Scenes From A Single Mom Blog* was born, with the intention to create the space and a community of women who could relate to being more than "just" a single mom—and demystify the "baby mama" stigma.

Today, When She Thrives programming includes The Scenes From A Single Mom Book Project, an opportunity for single moms to work in a cohort to reclaim their stories and pursue new goals as authors and entrepreneurs, S.O.A.R. (Successfully Overcoming Adversity with Resilience), and more.

Tiffany's resilience and resourcefulness is known to be a catalyst for changing lives after every single encounter. She is the founder and director of When She Thrives, a nonprofit with the mission to break generational cycles of single motherhood. She continues to counter grief with hope and reveals how the shame associated with society's stigmas and the masks we carefully maintain actually alienate us from our true selves and others. Tiffany's work and foundation capture the beautiful truths that are revealed as we courageously commit to reinventing ourselves in spite of it all.

Courageously committing is something Vera Anderson, legacy coach and founder of Global Elements consulting, did in the midst of her grief.

Vera shares, *"I experienced a profound loss in the market crash of 2008—not only business and financial—I lost my business partner of eight years to suicide. From that time, I have been on a personal quest to learn, heal and rise from that low. In doing so, I found myself continually seeking and growing toward my own full potential in business and as an individual.*

"What I've discovered is that life and its pressures and conflicting expectations can create unsustainable lifestyles and destructive belief systems. Everyone goes through this at some point in their work and life, but we don't always see it and are all affected differently. I have experienced this firsthand, working as an operating partner for a multinational manufacturing conglomerate, serving on boards of directors in three countries, and launching a number of other businesses.

"And what I've discovered is something I am passionate about sharing with others, applying what I've learned and tested for myself. My work has now become my legacy and empowers others in a profound way that helps them reach their full potential in their career and in business, live a fulfilling life, and enjoy rich relationships. My life's work is to help others intentionally create their own legacy and recognize and reach their fullest potential."

~*~

For She Who Grieves....

"Yes. This terrible thing happened. I am grieving it. I have grieved it. But I am also living. Life doesn't owe anyone a

happy ending just because they experienced something terrible. Including me. But I'm certain that happy days will exist. Happy moments. Happy feelings. I am choosing to allow space for happy. Some days are harder than others. I'll fake it until I make it. Some days are easier than others. I'll refuse to feel guilty for experiencing that too.

"It's a fine line, a sliver, where I balance experiencing grief and tucking it safely away so I can get through the day. I want to be real and acknowledge my pain, but I don't want to give it too much energy. But hope builds on a foundation that is strong, and strength comes from sharing grief. Some days it's easier to share my grief than others. Some days, I only want to look for joy.

"For she who grieves, the best is yet to come, even when we don't know what it will look like."

When some people grieve, their eyes spring open and affix on being a helping person. Grief is channeled into foundations, programs, projects. Some of the people whose stories inspired this book have created something powerful from the grief—here are a few of the foundations we've seen bring healing:

- The Little Fox Foundation, bringing SIDS awareness and safe sleep practices to families. The Little Fox was created in memory of Tobias "Toby" Graham Stern, who passed away on August 24, 2016, from SIDS. His parents, Katie and Dan Stern, created a 501(c)3 nonprofit in his memory. Toby's Foundation works to educate on the importance of safe sleep practices for infants, provides insight on sudden infant death syndrome (SIDS), and supports families (parents, siblings, grandparents, and extended family) who are grieving the loss of an infant. https://thelittlefoxfoundation.org/

- Rhett Sullivan Foundation is a nonprofit that aids families who experience unexpected early child loss with financial assistance, grief support, and resources. The loss of a young child is traumatic and touches many families within our community. The Foundation's goal is to provide relief in their time of need. Get involved at https://rhettsullivan.org/.
- Alina's Light is promoting the passing of Alina's Law (Pennsylvania House Bill 1747) to protect victims of domestic violence by giving the court a mechanism to enforce orders for protection from abuse (PFA). Alina's mom, Elly Sheykhet, is a certified grief coach, and her work is done in hopes that Alina's Law will save domestic violence victims from enduring further abuse or losing their lives to unchecked domestic violence. https://alinaslight.com/
- Center for Organ Recovery & Education (CORE) is one of 58 federally designated not-for-profit organ procurement organizations (OPOs) in the United States. CORE works closely with donor families and designated health care professionals to coordinate the surgical recovery of organs, tissues, and corneas for transplantation. CORE also facilitates the computerized matching of donated organs and placement of corneas. With headquarters in Pittsburgh, Pa., and an office in Charleston, W.Va.,

CORE oversees a region that encompasses 155 hospitals and almost six million people throughout western Pennsylvania, West Virginia, and Chemung County, N.Y. For more information, visit core.org or call 1-800-DONORS-7.

- When She Thrives empowers single moms to elevate their voices, reclaim their stories and become advocates for their families and communities https://www.whenshethrives.org/our-story.html
    - S.O.A.R. (Successfully Overcoming Adversity with Resilience) is a 12-week training program to equip single moms to advocate for both themselves and their families. The program is rooted at the intersection of self-care, social justice, and community building.
    - Visit https://www.whenshethrives.org/soar.html to learn more.
    - Growing Through Grants provides rapid-response, crisis-prevention grants to prevent hunger, homelessness, unemployment, or other potential crises when a family is faced with unexpected expenses. Visit https://www.whenshethrives.org/growing-through-grants.html to learn more.
- Global Elements Consulting, led by Vera Anderson, offers a dynamic and intentional experience to propel you to your next level of success, helping you reach your full potential in business and in life and leave a lasting legacy. Visit https://www.globalelementsconsulting.com/ to learn more.

It may be worth mentioning that just because you've been able to turn grief into hope and build something sturdy doesn't necessarily guarantee absolution and ensure safety from future trials. Actually, even if you may be a little more equipped to handle it, if the worst is waiting in the wings, it still hurts like hell. We've been there. Some of us a little bit more frequently or with more obvious intensity than others. In times like these, we've asked the following three questions:

What would have helped me?

Where can I help?

Who do I know that I can share this with?

Think it Out

What would you do with your grief to help others, if time and resources were not obstacles?

Which of these experiences resonates the most? Why?

How has your loss changed you? What would you like to continue to change?

Feel the Hope

Light a candle at a house of worship or in your very own home. The stories we shared are of people who became lights in the midst of their darkness.

The light always drives out the darkness.

Chapter 8: The Worst was Waiting in the Wings

"Grief ... gives life a permanently provisional feeling. It doesn't seem worth starting anything. I can't settle down. I yawn, I fidget, I smoke too much. Up till this, I always had too little time. Now there is nothing but time. Almost pure time, empty successiveness."

~ C.S. Lewis, *A Grief Observed*

Perhaps you know this provisional feeling. Familiarity with feeling unfamiliar with your body, your bed, your home, your job. Imagine going down to the basement, finding the big ol' box labeled "spring/summer clothes," and just as the sun starts to regularly peek through the clouds and flowers start to pop up all over, a wave of hope rushes over you. The days are getting longer, brighter. And you are feeling the warmth too. Maybe this is the day—the day that grief won't wrap you in a coldness that never seems to leave, and maybe this is the day that the anxiety that darkens the shades before the coffee gets poured doesn't awaken. Maybe this is the day.

So, slowly the spring/summer clothes are dragged up the stairs, and the lid is opened. The clothes are so inviting—

pale colors, soft fabrics, happier memories. You feel brave enough to try on one of those happier memories, indoors of course, because it isn't quite warm enough outside yet. All these clothes, your clothes, are laid out and ready for wearing. Daringly, pulling the first one overhead and on, you notice that the arms don't feel just right. Next. Pulling on the bottoms that once brought "luck" you thought ... zip. But they just feel all wrong. And so it goes. All these clothes fit. But nothing feels familiar. Those happier memories start fraying, even if the seams don't budge ...

"Getting over it so soon? But the words are ambiguous. To say the patient is getting over it after an operation for appendicitis is one thing; after he's had his leg off is quite another. After that operation, either the wounded stump heals or the man dies. If it heals, the fierce, continuous pain will stop. Presently he'll get back his strength and be able to stump about on his wooden leg. He has 'got over it.' But he will probably have recurrent pains in the stump all his life, and perhaps pretty bad ones; and he will always be a one-legged man. There will be hardly any moment when he forgets it. Bathing, dressing, sitting down and getting up again, even lying in bed, will all be different. His whole way of life will be changed. All sorts of pleasures and activities that he once took for granted will have to be simply written off. Duties too. At present I am learning to get about on crutches. Perhaps I shall presently be given a wooden leg. But I shall never be a biped again."

~ C.S. Lewis, *A Grief Observed*

The circumstances which lead to loss, and subsequently, grief, are often terrible things. Mixed up, moshed up, terrible things. When the circumstances include other people, revisiting the point of pain can have a paralyzing effect. Assigning blame to self or another is one way that some start to make sense of their grief. The unfamiliar feeling of grief and experience of loss just does not make sense any other way. By assigning blame, the idea is that there becomes a tangible outlet for these feelings. And where fault is found, forgiveness must be accompanied. This is never the easy part. For she who grieves, finding familiarity with feeling unfamiliar in her own body remains a reminder that fault and forgiveness are two "f" words that might be waiting in the wings.

"But miscarriage is a traumatic loss, not only of the pregnancy, but of a woman's sense of self and her hopes and dreams of the future. She has lost her 'reproductive story,' and it needs to be grieved," says Janet Jaffe, PhD, a clinical psychologist at the Center for Reproductive Psychology in San Diego and co-author of the 2010 book *Reproductive Trauma: Psychotherapy with Infertility and Pregnancy Loss Clients.*

For She Who Grieves...

"I remember reading these words as I numbly searched for something, anything, to help me understand what I was feeling, or what I should be feeling. Losing two babies in two years took more out of me than giving birth to two babies in two years just a few prior. Giving birth and raising children felt like the pinnacle of my adult womanhood. A string of unbreakable connection that I could share with my own mother and other women whose bodies experienced the same growth and birth. But the

circumstances around the first miscarriage broke the string and broke the part of me that had connected with my own childhood right along with it.

"It was very early in the morning, my family was barely stirring, when my mother called to tell me that he was finally going home. My long suffering father was slipping away. Immediately, I jumped in my vehicle and went to the place that I called home for the first two decades of my life. I didn't go there often, if at all. I had learned that people will choose what they know, and the family dynamics were not something that I wanted to expose my own children to. Years of exposure to substance abuse, heaps of lies, stunted development, and the broken spirit of someone close to my mother drove a wedge between me and those in the family who accepted the behavior. Wounded people behave differently than healthy folks, and I knew that I couldn't help or change the behaviors. So I created a wall, a boundary, a protective moat that kept my family far from the danger. Until my dad died. Until I thoughtlessly jumped in my car and drove right into the darkness and was confronted with the behaviors that I fled from.

"I should have listened to my gut.

"I should have stayed away.

"I should have ... well, I can't stay in the world of 'should have.' I have children to raise, work to do, and a life to live.

"Maybe what happened there wasn't what caused the miscarriage. But I'll never know because I didn't get back in my car and leave. Instead, I thought it was my duty to take care of my mother. I thought it was my duty to help her carry her grief. Even after being attacked by a monster. Even after hiding the calls to the police. Even after being told it was my fault. I should have stayed away.

"For days, and weeks, and months, I tried to fix the unfixable. Even as I was actively losing my child. Even as I was being told it was my fault. That I provoked him. Things would never be the same. That house would never be a place to go back to. That woman would never be the same person to me.

"Mourning death, mourning the living, and mourning the exact moment that I decided to drop down a boundary and enter into a space that was unsafe created a dynamic that I had to acknowledge eventually. But I wasn't ready. The thunder was only starting to roll through my life that summer. After losing my father, the first man to love me, and losing our child, whom I had yet to meet, my husband had a medical issue that required immediate attention. My grief needed to be suspended a bit longer.

"When we learned that my husband was facing a diagnosis of multiple sclerosis, our future and our present changed dramatically. There wasn't room for my grief. There wasn't room for my healing. There was only 'what's next.' What's the next medication to try? What's the next specialist to see? What's the next mood swing to navigate? Day after day, week after week, we kept moving into the

next phase. The grief didn't disappear, it just seeped in deeper and deeper. I tunneled it in, buried it up, and put on the brave face for the man whom I expected to spend the rest of my life with, even though I was terrified that it was going to be taken away. Grief for the living is no less difficult than grief for the dead.

"To counter the grief, we lived. We fought, we laughed, we prayed, we loved. We went on vacation! We invested in our children and in moments. We took inventory of what matters. We took advantage of good days. He left his job and stepped into a better opportunity with good people. I got a promotion. We moved forward, through the shock and grief, and pressed on. We chose to keep going. Time wasn't stopping, so how could we?

"By the time the next year rolled in, we experienced a miracle. We were expecting again. And there was just joy and expectation. Having a better handle on MS, and living in the boundaries that were established, this felt like a fresh start. I did everything perfectly. I was healthy. I maintained boundaries. I stayed calm. I stayed happy. And I lost the baby anyway. I felt the sting of failure. I felt the pain of loss. Checking into the hospital and checking out of hope ... it sucked. It was a couple of days before my 40th birthday. We had a huge party planned and I refused to cancel. Instead of grieving, I focused all of my energy on the physical element of healing. I slept until the ache was buried in my blankets.

"The loss of this child, so close to a milestone birthday, added to the pain that I was unsure of how to acknowledge. Holding the grief of both mother and child

at the same time still feels like sand slipping through my fingers. It's not just that I lost one baby. Or two. But in many ways, I also lost my mother. And these feelings that stayed unresolved are all wrapped up together and tied with a barbed wire bow."

"The tragedy of miscarriage has traditionally been private, an event grieved largely by the mother, on her own. Health-care professionals advised these women that the sadness would grow less pronounced over time, especially following a successful pregnancy" (Newman, 2012).

As She Grieves ...

"Today, as I write this, I'm not fully recovered. I've maintained commitment to the habits that help me, particularly physical movement and walking miles and miles every day. I've reintroduced habits that bring me peace like reading and praying the rosary. I've allowed for those carefully curated boundaries to build up protective walls around my home, my family unit, and my emotional well-being. I've mustered up the courage to talk about it when I need to and allow myself to cry if I need to. I hear the voice of the lie that my grief is shameful and respond back to it with the truth that I am resilient.

"Mourning the living while I honor the dead is now part of the journey that I'm on."

What She Needs ...

Affirmation that this is normal, too. Space to grieve. Reminders that without this, she would not be who she is today, and she is resilient and strong enough to be vulnerable.

The nature of some grief is such that life doesn't stop, so it gets filed away or packed up and stored like seasonal clothing. The grief is one thing, but finding a way to forgive through the hurting and healing is another.

For she who grieves, the forgiveness doesn't come without a measure of fortitude. Releasing the trauma and being brave are works seldom done alone.

On Forgiveness

Forgiveness is often part of releasing trauma and coping with grief and can aid in healing. True forgiveness is one of the most important and liberating steps you will ever experience, allowing you to get free from any person or situation having power over you.

By releasing the hurt of what another person has done, we experience freedom. Have you felt this? If we are still carrying hurt from other people, they still essentially control us. When you release the hurt, the emotional connection with that person is also released. This can be a very good thing.

Newsflash: True forgiveness is never about justifying someone's behavior or giving them the okay to keep being horrible. It doesn't mean you're okay with what they've done. It's not about releasing someone from being accountable for their actions; it's about releasing your pain around it. Forgiveness doesn't mean what that person did wasn't bad; it just means you're letting it go so the negativity around it doesn't weigh you down.

True organic forgiveness is for YOU, not for the other person.

For She Who Grieves ...

"To paraphrase what I heard from a talk by Scarlett Lewis, mom of a first grader murdered in the Sandy Hook Elementary School (Sandy Hook, Conn.) tragedy in 2012: Forgiveness isn't a gift you give to another person; it's for YOU! It's a gift you give yourself—it's freedom from anger and pain. It's not about letting the person off the hook. It's a choice: this is what I want for myself, then a process of forgiving again and again each time the anger comes up (starting with, 'I am open to the idea of forgiveness'). It's not about doing it all at once. You'll fall back. That's okay. Just cut the cord again. You might do that process for the rest of your life. It's a super power. It's simple (cutting that cord), not necessarily easy. It doesn't mean you condone what they've done or that you're not holding them accountable." (Lewis, 2021)

Hurt people hurt people. Sometimes viewing the person that way, that they are acting out of pain, helps with forgiveness. You are not condoning what was done. You are simply acknowledging the reality that horrible shit happens, and we are all human.

Sometimes a misunderstanding around what forgiveness is about makes processing grief more difficult.

For She Who Grieves ...

"This was an important realization for me. You hear about how important forgiveness is to move on. I always grew up thinking that forgiveness was about relieving someone else of their pain and shame and wrongdoing. I thought forgiveness was about accepting that what someone did was ok for whatever reason. And it was about me understanding them and justifying their choices with rationale.

"So, for me, I really struggled with forgiving a person for purposely hurting me, for intentionally punishing me despite my own remorse. Even though I could forgive to some degree if I thought of this person as hurt, for some reason, that kind of forgiveness didn't seem to have any benefits. Especially because I was continually exposed to this person hurting me over and over and over again. It wasn't a situation where I could forgive and forget and move on. The violations were continuing in a different form and a different level because we had a different relationship now. I was continually being confronted with boundary breaking, gaslighting, threats; just when I thought I could forgive, I would be confronted with another violation. I could never get ahead of it.

"Another aspect of forgiveness that I have been told is important was to either write it and give it to the person, or let them know in person that you were forgiving them. In my situation, I could not bring myself to do that. Logically I understood the value of that. Intuitively, something was telling me not to do that. Even though one form of therapy was telling me the best thing I should do

is tell this person I forgave them, thank God a different therapist told me, 'In your situation it is not safe mentally, let alone physically, to forgive someone who is continually mistreating you. It is extremely disempowering. By telling them that you forgive them, or even that you are sorry for hurting them, you are handing your power over to them, and that is what they thrive on. You are feeding the beast. ***You do not need to forgive this person in that way.****'*

"That statement in and of itself was empowering for me. It gave me relief. My intuition was telling me that it wasn't right, and it was validating. In my situation, it could have made things worse.

"When I looked more into forgiveness, because I did still have unresolved feelings, I realized that forgiveness isn't for them; it's for you. It's for me. It's for me to come to terms in some way. The idea of forgiveness is to empower yourself, not the other person. Forgiveness won't change what happened, but it will change the outcome. The outcome I desire is peace and hope restored. The present outcome I have is enlightenment. The work I will continue to do doesn't end here, even if the experience of grief becomes more distant."

Maybe you need to forgive others when they cannot understand your lived experience, like our other friend.

"Some people find peace and give themselves permission to do what I did, because I'm providing the example. Others look at me like the cruelest person on the planet— 'It's your MOM!' With those types of people, I always say

to myself, 'They're just not your audience.' I meet people where they are. So I never let their views or perception of my situation impact how I felt; I'm not mad or frustrated with them. They just don't understand. It's hard to relate unless you've been through that. I can't hold that against them."

Or maybe, you need to forgive yourself.

Think it Out

What is your experience of forgiveness and being forgiven?

What might you want to forgive yourself for?

What does forgiving yourself look like?

What are the risks or rewards in the work of forgiving?

How does one (or should one ever) forgive the unforgivable?

What is the difference between forgiveness and release?

What does forgiveness look like, as it relates to your experience or after-effects of grief?

Feel the Hope

Shed what doesn't suit you any longer. Go through your own seasonal clothing and remove what no longer works for who you are and where you are. Release those items by giving them away to create opportunity for someone else.

Chapter 9: Releasing Trauma and Being Brave

Disasters happen every day. All over the globe. Earthquakes. Hurricanes. Tornados. Tsunamis. Hunger. Housefires. Trainwrecks. Plane crashes. Floods. Droughts. Haboobs. Blizzards. And a whole myriad of less globally pervasive tragedies. As human beings experience these things, and escape with relatively few physical injuries, another injury often lies beneath the surface. Triggered by loud noises, different smells, certain rooms, and other commonalities of daily life, survivors of disaster and tragedy carry with them an invisible hitch hiker, Trauma. We've mentioned "trauma" a number of times up until now, but "Trauma" deserves a moment all her own to receive the attention we try so desperately to ignore.

The relationship between Trauma and Grief can be complicated. Think of it like this—although both are normal reactions to the difficult moments of life, trauma demands a different response than grief. Grief can be a companion, a welcome companion even, where Trauma is a life-sucking vampire. Trauma willingly paralyzes her victims. Grief has the capacity to turn a widow into a warrior.

Trauma ought to be autopsied and never laid to rest. Pulled apart, deconstructed, and finally and carefully disempowered. That's where the healing comes from. In releasing trauma, and becoming brave, grief changes in energy.

People want a step-by-step process for grief relief and releasing sorrow and pain. We're sorry to say that there isn't one. Not a universal one anyway. To move from grief to a positive force, and to create a present place of peace, there's only one thing to do: *You have to feel to heal.*

Not all trauma is commonly shared, like a community embracing each other to weather a hurricane. Some trauma is concealed. The trauma experienced by those who have experienced abuse of any kind may be accompanied by something else, preventing it from being looked at in broad daylight. Some trauma is experienced in a different time and place and is easy to lock away in a closet, forgotten. Some trauma exists not because of anything that has happened *to* us but because we witnessed something so unexpected that sorting through the emotions is difficult.

Sometimes the most fascinating and engaging people carry with them the deepest traumas, and potentially un-triaged wounds. This is true for some of the women who inspired this book and who shared their stories—so many stories picking apart the unimaginable circumstances and revealing the warrior woman who is clothed in bravery as she steps forward with grief as an accomplice, not an assassin.

What was the first step one friend took to become the warrior she is? She shares ...

"You may have to take a moment to have a pity party and get all the emotional energy out, and you have to release that energy to get through it.

"Even though I said, 'Enough is enough,' and 'Go kill yourself,' I was mad, and then I immediately cried. I lost my mother that day. I literally cried uncontrollably, exhaustingly cried, and let it all go then. Then I did it again when I gave her the ultimatum of, 'Do this or this will happen.'

"But when you let that all out, you'll realize the strength is there; it's just the emotion is over top of it. If you can't let the grief out, your strength can't rise up."

The compounded grief she experienced demanded a release. The experience of relationship violence, coupled with the "death" of the woman who raised her, shook our friend to the core. It wasn't just one grief to feel and heal, it stirred up years of moments and memories that flooded the carefully cultivated life that was already hanging by a thread. Sound familiar? Different circumstances, but similar experiences for many of us, huh?

Another friend shares a different but similarly complicated experience ...

For She Who Grieves ...

"'Abuse' is a general yet heavy word. I don't like it. Most people cringe. I do. I have a really hard time using it related to what I experienced and a person I really thought I knew and loved. 'Domestic violence,' 'relationship violence,' 'intimate partner violence,' whatever the term, they are all cringey ... sharp and harsh words, especially to those who have experienced any of it; yet often clouded with fuzz, especially if it didn't happen like how it does on TV. So many gray, muddled concepts. What do you call ongoing invasion of privacy and security in one's home that results in understandable paranoia? Is sleep-deprivation torture considered physical abuse? What if the perpetrator is traumatized? When does coercion through intimidation and threats cross the line? Why does this all depend on the state in which you live?! It gets complicated.

"Yet, a blend of complicated abuse and complex trauma was my experience ... Sudden, then drawn out for an intense period; so surreal, often covert, so unbelievable and distorted that I didn't even know what I was experiencing at the time. Even though, to my therapists, it was clear. In addition to living in fear and constant confusion during that crisis, I was living in shock and denial."

Grief can certainly be found in trauma. Grief and trauma alone are each difficult. Trauma and loss together is a doozy—whether the trauma and/or loss (of relationship, of self, or of control for example) is sudden, extended, or repeated over time, whether it is abuse or death or deformity or witnessing or experiencing a horrific event.

If that's not enough, there's also something called "traumatic grief," a relatively new term for grief that happens in response to a sudden, unexpected loss. For example, maybe you lost a child, or experienced the violent death of someone close to you. The terms "traumatic grief" and "complicated grief" used to be used interchangeably, but since the attacks on the United States on September 11, 2001, "traumatic grief" has been reserved for the psychological reaction following a traumatic event and for grief following the loss of a person during such an event (Bifulco, 2007). Traumatic grief is more likely to lead to complicated grief.

Not every sudden or catastrophic loss results in traumatic grief. Some people experience uncomplicated bereavement. But others may show signs of both trauma and grief. While bereavement, or devastation from the death of a loved one, has been cited as one of the most traumatic life events (Milik et al., 2017), traumatic grief is different from the grief that happens from an expected loss, such as when someone passes away after a long chronic illness. The feelings that come with traumatic grief are much more intense. That doesn't mean that other forms of grief are any less difficult to deal with.

"The shock and unexpected nature of the loss can be traumatizing and trigger intrusive, preoccupying thoughts or bodily responses that are essentially distorted survival mechanisms in addition to the mourning of whatever was unexpectedly lost," says Michael Roeske, Psy.D. and executive director at Newport Healthcare Connecticut. "PTSD relating to grief is also especially likely if you have an existing mental health condition at the time you experience a traumatic loss," adds Roeske (Coehlo & Johnson, 2022). If you're living with depression, for example, you may have a more pronounced reaction to a loss.

Glenda Dickonson, a licensed clinical professional counselor in private practice in Maryland, describes traumatic grief as "a sense-losing event—a free fall into a chasm of despair." Because of the trauma embedded within the grief, it can be challenging to differentiate between PTSD, grief, and traumatic grief. "PTSD is about fear, and grief is about loss. Traumatic grief will have both, and it includes a sense of powerlessness," Dickonson explains. "A person who is experiencing traumatic grief becomes a victim—a victim of the trauma in addition to the loss. [...] They will assume those qualities of experiencing trauma even while grieving the loss" (Phillips, 2021)

Alright, alright, enough already. We'd like to pause for a reminder of intention here. This is not meant to be a diagnostic manual or comprehensive guide to grief, or trauma, but a collection of stories and researched information that presents a deep and sensitive, broad and informative view of grief, and one we hope offers insight and ideas to those seeking understanding, meaning, and consideration.

It is not meant to explain every type of experience so you can classify yours or anyone else's, as tempting as that might be. We want to make sure that is clear. Please don't let types, labels, categories, or definitions detract from the heart of the matter: Everyone's story matters. Your story matters. Traumatic or not. Consider the references and stories herein to expand your view and open your mind and, mainly, your heart. Now that we've had that gentle pause, let's talk about ...

Perpetuating Crap

We have talked about how trauma, grief and PTSD can affect your brain. Unknowingly and unfortunately, we often perpetuate our own traumas in the ways we relate to ourselves. Let that sink in. It's not enough to just experience crap once, but we keep rerunning the episode? Sometimes.

What we've learned, in digging deep into our own grief work and poring over tomes of research, data, and thought leadership is that in childhood, for example, not being heard, might set up our relationship with ourselves as an adult for emotionally ignoring ourselves, until we heal this. A belief explained by many trauma champions and other experts is that many of us have unconscious, unhealed wounds, especially before around age 8, that make us vulnerable to repeated harmful experiences.

It's a good time to reiterate something of paramount importance about some of these thought leaders. What we've discovered is that the voices bringing comfort and clarity to the grief work we've embarked on have come to create a collective chorus for us—words and phrases discovered at one point have matriculated so much so that they begin to blend seamlessly with other thoughts and discoveries. We'll continue to do our best to point you toward these thought leaders, even if only in passing, so the healing balm covers the most tender parts of the grief-to-hope journey, like it has for us. The Helpful Considerations & Resources section at the end of this book mentions a few.

Unhealed wounds and traumas can lead to false or limiting beliefs that can keep us stuck in bad patterns or stall our healing. Unconscious beliefs like "I'm not worth it," "I can't succeed," "Crying is bad," or "People I love hurt me," can thwart our progress, potential, and personal fulfillment. Consider if beliefs created from someone else's criticism, rage, stress, betrayal, or abuse are running a script in the background of your being. Or maybe the beliefs stem from a really unfortunate but heavy, harmful experience.

Have you ever asked yourself if a thought you are struggling with is based on a belief about yourself, and whether that belief is actually based in fact? Orrrr, why you even hold a certain belief about *yourself*? Ever made a list of evidence for if it's true or why it's not? Ever realized a new belief is in order? You reroute your neural pathway by evaluating, reframing, and practicing new, more appropriate beliefs.

Stick with us on this, because releasing the trauma requires an investigation of offenses. It's the only way. We recommend pausing for a moment to consider whether seeking a professional to guide you through some of this would be helpful at this time. Professional therapists and counselors offer a wide variety of mechanisms to work through trauma, and if you are recognizing some indications that more exploration is needed for your own healing, by all means, put the book down and make the call.

Here are some quick references, just in case:

Text HOME to 741741 from anywhere in the United States, anytime. Crisis Text Line is here for any crisis. A live, trained crisis counselor receives the text and responds, all from their secure online platform. The volunteer crisis counselor will help you move from a hot moment to a cool moment.

The National Alliance on Mental Illness (NAMI) HelpLine can be reached Monday through Friday, 10 a.m. – 10 p.m., ET.

Call 1-800-950-NAMI (6264), text "HelpLine" to 62640

National Domestic Violence Hotline: Text "START" to 88788 or call 1-800-799-7233. Anyone who is experiencing domestic violence and/or abuse, plus anyone concerned about a friend, family member or loved one can call the National Domestic Violence Hotline 24 hours a day, seven days a week.

National Suicide Prevention Lifeline call 1-800-273-TALK (8255)

Call or text 988 Suicide & Crisis Lifeline. The Lifeline provides 24/7 free and confidential support for people in distress, prevention and crisis resources for you or your loved ones, and best practices for professionals in the United States.

For She Who Grieves ...

"When I was a young teen, my mother read my diary. She was at her wits' end, concerned for my behavior and worried that I had fallen in with a risky crowd. I had. Still, that violation devastated me. I was at a very vulnerable age, and I felt embarrassed and humiliated by all the deeply personal thought and emotion I had poured into that diary, and ashamed for the troublesome behavior I had engaged in. It was unclear all she read, but I felt like my conscience had been ripped out and my most private Freudian thoughts exposed with it. I could no longer hug my mother, although she didn't give up and was very sorry for hurting me that way, and I knew she loved me very much.

"It's quite possible that from that significant experience I formed a subconscious belief: that it's okay for people close to you to cross your boundaries when it's out of love, and you need to forgive them because they did it out of care and concern, because YOU were doing something wrong. So, it was forgivable, if not acceptable, for them to have done what they did."

We all have "stuff." It's part of growing up, part of our self-development. Even with the best parents and life on earth, we're going to have experiences that form our beliefs about ourselves and the world, right or wrong. Bottom line: As an adult, you are responsible for you. Ultimately, you are responsible for the choices you make. You can choose to discover what is and isn't serving you. You can choose to release and shift a belief. You have to take personal responsibility to create the life you want.

"That said, that same age-old experience served to guide me out of a relationship crisis, years later. During the reconciliation process, my partner encouraged me to process my thoughts on paper, and when I would offer to share them, in the spirit of full transparency, my partner would refuse. This person knew of my past diary drama and how devastating that was to me. So when I found out this same person was reading my personal notes behind my back and using the information to test my honesty while I thought we were so earnestly working on our relationship, I was cut to the core.

"My original belief may have led me to forgive that impasse at the time, because I felt so guilty about my part in our situation, but eventually, after several months of couples counseling, I discovered long-term, ongoing digital surveillance via computer spyware and voice recorders. I was completely dumbfounded and felt absolutely eviscerated. In choosing to share that particular situation and my re-devastation with my personal therapist, and even with my mother, I realized I was holding a belief that needed major modification. They helped me recognize that this kind of behavior was not acceptable even in the most loving relationships; in fact, my mother was the most adamant. The incident became yet another factor in my decision to leave."

The emotional trauma exists. The emotional wounds are just as real and important to recognize as the physical ones. And oh, by the way, ignoring our wounds does not heal them.

According to Melanie Tonia Evans, narcissistic abuse recovery expert, “we cannot heal what we are not prepared to feel.” Melanie runs programs focused on healing at the emotional, energetic level so people can thrive, not just survive. There is growing conviction that self-partnering and meeting and releasing traumas and making unconscious wounds conscious is necessary and often long overdue.

Melanie created a Quantum Freedom Healing modality, which:

> teaches you how to turn inwards and feel and hold and load up your traumas, release them cellularly, bring in source, which is your higher self, which has the power to heal what we logically can’t. This is what grants you the shift in your somatic, visceral body, which means that once you get that shift, you dissolve your peptide addictions to more trauma and your brain synapsis wiring gets an immediate shift as well (Evans, 2020).

For She Who Grieves...

“I wish I had learned sooner that I was trying to heal an emotional experience mostly intellectually, and that can only go so far. I had great success once I started focusing on my experience as trauma and PTSD. The crisis agency was a huge help with that. EMDR (eye movement desensitization and processing) was a big boost for me. A quantum science-based way of releasing traumatic energy stuck in our limbic system was ultimately the clincher. This conscious-subconscious process entails

healing old wounds and beliefs by tracing where they came from and imagining the release of dense energy stuck in our bodies. I have let go of so much pain, and my life perspective has broadened and deepened. I know it sounds woo woo but it's really oh wow!"

A number of doctors, scientists, and human transformation practitioners like Melanie, such as Joe Dispenza, Judith Orloff, Bruce Lipton, and Bessel van der Kolk are part of this emerging field exploring quantum science and the mind-body connection. Much has been said both in past and recent history about the power of one's mindset and how much the brain can control the body.

New neuroscience is shifting the idea that if we change our thinking, we can change our somatic, emotional response (the brain controls the body) to the other way around: the body controls the brain. A growing scientific theory is, by working on your emotional self first, your brain will automatically follow what you feel. How you feel is how you're going to think. So how you are programmed viscerally, energetically, is how you're going to show up and dictates your belief system on a bodily level. Think about it: our choices have to do with how we feel and our beliefs.

Some of us have spent so much time trying to think our way out of significant trauma, to understand and rationalize our situation and manage our feelings logically, and it just hasn't worked. At least not fast enough. Has it worked for you? As we've purported, understanding and clarity is important to a degree of course, and there are definitely helpful ways to foster hope and healing. But has all the thinking you've done and discussions you've had healed you?

If not, consider the idea that maybe to change your reality and the way you think, you have to change the way you feel. Maybe understanding aspects of the brain-body connection and what they mean for you is most important. Maybe, to change the way you feel, you have to release your trauma, and reprogram it with something healthier. Why not turn inward and create some space in your Self—something we actually have some more control over that has rippling personal benefits?

Maybe quantum healing is not for you; it's not for everybody. Just know that it has proven to help many and is something to consider for your toolbox. We like the idea of healing from the inside out, along with having practical strategies to help guide us in the right direction. It's much more empowering and self-solidifying than focusing on medicating symptoms or blaming the cause of our suffering on another person or harping on ourselves. Yes, understanding that another person brought it on or activated it can be validating, but your own feelings and beliefs are driving your current state, many of them unconsciously. Part of being present is gaining consciousness of your own Self!

For She Who Grieves...

"'I'm not like other people,' when it comes to betrayal and revenge, my partner warned me early on. Ironically, I ended up hurting them right where it seemed their past trauma lay: betrayal. When I finally left, I enacted what

was likely their greatest fear: abandonment. Crazy how life works. The important piece here, along with that now bright-red, high flying, literal warning flag, is how they chose to react.

"My partner could've been angry and let me go. They could've been distraught and faced their demons. They could have honestly and genuinely decided to work with me and their emotions. Instead, it was as though they essentially kept me around to toy with and punish.

"In their grief, they chose revenge. Over hope. Over love. Maybe they tried. But revenge won out. They ended up self-fulfilling their prophecy, and losing what supposedly mattered most: me."

As She Grieves ...

"To deal with my grief, over the years I have discovered several ways to heal emotionally. Sometimes the experience of grief responds better to different things at different times. Talking about it was crucial; it can take time to find the right therapist, but I consider that essential. I've tried all sorts of therapies like CBT (cognitive behavioral therapy), EMDR, EFT, craniosacral therapy, acupuncture, various forms of meditation, medication, self-development classes, books, blogs, vitamins and supplements, daily affirmations, the 12 steps (for anger addiction), quality conversations with trusted individuals, lots of crying, re-reading journals and notes ... sheeesh ...

What She Needs ...

"Those all contributed to my healing. With time and intellectual, emotional, and even biological processing, I have released so much of the grief and trauma. With the biggest shifts, my strange somatic symptoms—which mimicked several other diseases, that no doctor has been able to figure out for years—have oddly disappeared. It's amazing really. My hyper-vigilance and hyper-sensitivity have finally mellowed, I am triggered less readily, and I know how to cope in the moment.

"I have gained confidence in my perceptions, intuition, emotions, insights, and decisions. I am stronger, wiser, bolder, more uniquely sensitive, and more soul-nourishing, self-aware, and self-advocating."

What if we reframed our approach to trauma like our friend here, by incorporating a modality that allows us to take our power back by turning inward, with kindness, self-love, and care? What if, instead of "coping" and "surviving," we leveraged grief and trauma to consciously grow and thrive?

Try this: "*From today onward, I take my power back and accept that the wounds inside me are mine and only I can heal them. By doing so, I can and will set myself free.*" Focus on this and your healing, rather than any perpetrator and what happened.

When you are struggling to let go of pain, to break down the resistance and painful inner battle in the moment, you can try, "*I trust and accept this feeling.*" Replace any victimization process with a blessing and some self-compassion. That allows hope to gently flow into your experience. It is all part of the human experience, to feel the good and the bad, the happy and sad. It is part of our evolution.

More for the Open-Minded

We all will face life-shattering events and incredible pain at some point. To create a better present and a more exciting future, consider learning the value of releasing negative past experiences and transforming your way of thinking.

You may have heard about someone at an extreme low point in their life, realizing that there must be something bigger going on. It happens. Have you ever felt like, “This can’t all be for nothing”? Would you consider making a firm decision: “No matter how bad my situation is, I am willing to overcome it”? Try it! And see, maybe there is something in store for you.

There’s more to experiencing inner peace, of course, but it starts with the realization that in every situation lies a space to make a choice (there’s that “choice” word again!). If your painful emotions are being fed by your thoughts, and your thoughts are just choices, maybe you could choose to change your thinking about the event.

Crystal McFadden, speaker, coach, and licensed professional counselor, is also a proponent of cognitive flexibility and reframing for navigating the hard stuff. When you change your point of view of a situation, the meaning changes, and thinking and behavior often change along with it. She learned that the hardships in her life had great power when she reframed them. In 2021, she facilitated an experience for a group of women in which we participated, and she encouraged us to literally draw a horizontal line to mark our individual major life experiences and milestones on. This timeline activity is commonly used when working to reframe one's view of their personal history.

With Crystal's instruction, we went a step further, making a three-column list to categorize 1) Experiences—"the things that happened *to* me" (from the timeline), 2) Choices—"what I actually chose to do or avoid," and 3) Outcomes—"what happened next." This activity allowed each of us to gain a new perspective. That sounds easy, right? It wasn't. Sometimes, to gain a new perspective about a personally complex entanglement of emotions, we have to be confronted with this unavoidable truth: personal history matters.

Try this for yourself. In this particular exercise, allow grief to be the underlying theme that you are exploring as you build the timeline. Work to answer these questions as you explore:

- Who did you meet?
- What skill did you learn?
- Did you gain certain insight that equipped you well?
- What lessons did you learn?
- What strengths did you develop?
- Did this thing that happened build your character?
- Look over and across your list. Does a theme emerge?

Using your personal timeline to prepare the list allows you an opportunity to recognize the choices you have made and the impact they have had. Framing your thinking in a new way can change your response—the way you think, feel and behave—and your ability to rise above! Do you believe this? Do you believe that you can change your response?

Megan Wollerton, health coach, trainer, athlete, and owner of Life Force Wellness, also promotes the value of reframing limiting beliefs in her wellness practice, often drawing from Carol Dweck's renowned research on mindset and other well-known models of resiliency, such as those from Dr. Aldo Pucci. During a talk in 2022, she suggested we ask ourselves Pucci's "three rational questions" (2006).

- Is my thinking based on fact?
- Does my thinking help me achieve my goal?
- Does it help me feel the way I want to feel?

Three "yes" answers means your thought is rational and you should keep it. It works for you. One or more "no" answers means that your thought is irrational, and it's in your best interest to replace it with a healthier, more realistic thought.

Another approach is to consider evidence for your belief. Megan encourages asking yourself the following questions, also drawn from cognitive behavior therapy techniques:

- Why am I holding this belief?
- What evidence do I have for why it's true?

Make two lists—Why it's true and Why it's not—and evaluate the evidence. Which list is larger? You may find that a belief is against your values. You may find you have been exaggerating something unnecessarily. You can reestablish the neural network by practicing a reframed belief.

Here are some additional suggestions found to be helpful from some of our contributors and adapted and modified from other sources like *Life After Trauma: A Workbook for Healing* (Rosenbloom 1999).

- If you're having a hard time, it's ok to stop what you are doing and make choices to take care of yourself. Try to approach it from the perspective of, "I'm not here to fix. I'm here to find and reconnect with something whole in myself."
- Just be still and silent for a moment.
- Pay attention to how your body feels. Release the tension in your shoulders, jaw, stomach.
- Breathe. Easily. Deeply. Slowly. In through your nose, out through your mouth.
- Locate the physical sensation from the emotional discomfort and breathe into it, with your hand on that space.
- Identify the feeling associated with the sensation. Don't get caught up in the drama of the story. Let thoughts pass in and out. Just focus on the feeling. Rock or sway if you need to. It can be hard to feel. Focus on the feeling, not the circumstances.

- If your eyes are closed, it's okay to open your eyes and look around to help you feel more grounded. Try, "I bless and accept this feeling." Cry.
- Picture the feeling in a bubble, "Thank you. I love you. You served your purpose. It's time for you to be free." Let it float away for the universe to recycle into something beautiful.
- Say to yourself, "It's ok. I'm here. And I will never leave you."

Consider what belief a trauma in your life created that isn't true? That isn't serving you anymore? What old dead-end pattern exists that can be replaced with new hopeful behavior? What message do you need to send your amygdala?

- Instead of, "I'm not safe" or "I can't trust myself," try, "I knew it was not okay, and I left."
- Instead of, "I don't know what's real," focus on the facts.
- Instead of emphasizing the negative in yourself, affirm your attributes.
- Instead of withdrawing emotionally, try setting boundaries.
- Instead of worrying about the future, focus on making positive changes now.
- Rather than avoiding intimate relationships, take a step toward trusting a friend.
- If you're afraid to express your needs, practice speaking up with safe, supportive people.

Hope comes from and allows functioning in more expansive ways. Consider identifying a belief or behavior pattern that keeps you down. Over the next few months, practice substituting it with a more freeing one. When you feel good about that, begin shifting another pattern. Give each one some time to make progress. Any step to exercise your hope muscle is a step to heal your heart. Think this stuff is neat? So did millions of others who picked up *Emotional Freedom* from Judith Orloff. We didn't make it up—well some of it we did, based on experience, but first we turned to the experts, and we hope that you follow the references to this book and other resources and do the same.

There is much to be said about positive thinking and mindset, beliefs, attitudes, energy, and emotions. It doesn't have to be complicated. Let's take two basics we are all naturally equipped with: laughter and crying (yes, we are reframing crying to be positive!).

Laughter may be the Best Medicine

Like grief, laughter transcends cultural, age, and gender boundaries. Like grief, it also serves a social function, and can affect our health. Laughter may seem inappropriate or the last thing you feel like doing when grieving or healing from trauma; just know when you find humor in something, there's a whole lot of health benefits that come with it.

Laughter can increase your oxygen intake and stimulate your heart, lungs and muscles, and the effects on our heart rate and blood pressure are ultimately calming and tension-relieving. Laughter produces endorphins, those feel-good brain chemicals (also released when exercising by the way) that help relieve pain and stress. Laughter can even boost our immune system response with the release of stress and illness-reducing neuropeptides (Stierwalt 2020).

Elle Woods, from the movie *Legally Blonde*, sums up the effects of endorphins nicely: "Exercise gives you endorphins. Endorphins make you happy. Happy people just don't kill their husbands" (Luketic, 2001). Husbands everywhere applaud this.

The best part is that laughter signals cooperation, a key aspect of human survival; it's a way for us to signal to another person that we wish to connect. Not only does it promote a healthier body; laughter connects us. It helps us realign with joy.

"Even when I was blubbering and sobbing and horrified at my own condition, my concerned best friend's genuinely horrified yet ridiculously animated reaction got me snorting and choking on giggles between sobs. She didn't know it, but she looked just like a wacky Muppet we used to watch on TV when we were little. Once I shared that with her, we about peed our pants."

Friends are great for keeping things light sometimes. Grief and mourning doesn't have to be heavy and tense all the time. Friends are great for getting a break and having fun, and allowing the opportunity for talking about grief—if a person wants to. It doesn't have to be brought up; let the person talk about their loss at their own pace. Good friends are people you might want to talk about things with, but you also want to be with them because they are people you're still connected to.

"When I was younger, and was formulating my opinions about death, I made it clear to my family and friends that if I ever was in the hospital on my deathbed, to bring me Saturday Night Live *videos. I knew, even then, that laughter is the best medicine for me."*

Some people feel better when they laugh. Of course, humor may be unwelcome at certain times. We aren't saying this is the remedy to all ills, but in our experience, humor seems to compete with negative thoughts by inserting positive ones.

"I saw grief drinking a cup of sorrow and called out, 'It tastes sweet, does it not?' 'You've caught me,' grief answered, 'and you've ruined my business. How can I sell sorrow when you know it's a blessing?' ~ Jalāl al-Dīn Rūmī

Crying is the Best Home Remedy

Ok so again, maybe not the best remedy for all pain. But it sure can feel as good as a soothing cup of coffee, or even laughing. And crying, like laughing, is innate, and also has health benefits (Newhouse 2021). Crying too releases endorphins (endogenous opioids like oxytocin) that ease both physical and emotional pain and can actually help improve your mood! Emotional tears release stress hormones and other toxins, so your stress level lowers, which can help you sleep better and strengthen your immune system. And, like laughing, crying has been shown to increase connection, encouraging closeness, empathy, and support from friends and family.

Can you feel the energy of grief begging for release? Crying can make you feel better, even when pain persists. Psychologists note the value of crying when it comes to avoiding repressive coping, which, as we know with unresolved trauma, can have negative effects on our health. Keeping difficult feelings inside can be linked to a less resilient immune system, cardiovascular disease and hypertension, and stress, anxiety, and depression. In the prolific writings of Sigmund Freud, the encouragement to experience, explore, and externalize emotion is found. He states, "Unexpressed emotions will never die. They are buried alive and will come forth is uglier ways" (Freud et al., 1953). Find a safe place to let it out! Get rid of the false conception that crying is weak. Crying is healthy.

Of course, there are times when crying can be a sign of a problem, especially if it happens very frequently and/or for no apparent reason, or when crying starts to affect daily activities or becomes uncontrollable. Conversely, people suffering from certain kinds of clinical depression may actually *not* be able to cry, even when they feel like it. In any of these situations, it would be best to see a medical professional who can help diagnose the problem and suggest appropriate treatment.

People grieve in different ways. Not everyone will cry or feel sad when they grieve. Sometimes people cry tears of joy. Just know that you can embrace the laughter. And the tears. And the grief. It can be a sign of healing.

Living this New Life

"Feeling like I haven't been able to fully share my story has delayed my healing to some degree. It's not all rosy; I do still deal with anxiety and fragmented thinking. Depression looms like the ghost of grief. I'm still on my journey after all, but I am conscious now that the psychological, neurological and biochemical effects of what I experienced have been holding me back from living my best life. I'm changing all that."

The acceptance that life is different, and that you are different, is part of making the choice to keep moving. The famous words of Helen Keller ring effectively true at this moment, "Life is either a daring adventure or nothing" (1940). It may not feel very adventurous to muster up all your effort to put on your sneakers and take a walk around the neighborhood, but it truly is! This new life must be lived. This life, as it is, will be forever different from life as we wished it would be. Every day, for the rest of time and eternity, is life as it is. Not life as we thought it would be. Not life as we hoped it would be. Not life as we wanted it to be. So, living this new life is your new job.

Sometimes the body, on the outside, and the spirit, take a minute to sync up. The practice of walking—not just across the kitchen to the freezer to snag another pint of ice cream or glass of ice and vodka—but really walking for more than twenty minutes has this effect. It forces the body to move. The heart to pump blood. The lungs to breathe oxygen in and out of the body. All this movement, all these involuntary and automatic actions, does something. We've shared so much science with you, so we will spare you on the physiological effects of walking daily (they are great though!). We will even spare you the psychological and psychosomatic effects. Aren't we kind, here toward the end?

"I drank because I wanted to drown my sorrows, but now the damned things have learned to swim." ~ Frida Kahlo (Herrera, 1983)

The effect of walking daily that we *will* share ... it moves grief. Living life as it is, walking in the shoes she owns, breathing the air her body pushes through, on the roads she knows, our friend claims that she was able to keep moving through grief and was able to do something every day—even if it was just one thing, like walking. "*The work of walking seemed a whole lot less intimidating than packing up the baby clothes that were in the nursery, unused ...*" This something, as simple as it seemed, gave hope.

"Yesterday is but a dream, and tomorrow is only a vision, but today well lived makes every yesterday a dream of happiness and every tomorrow a vision of hope." ~ Khalil Gibran

Life as it is isn't always pretty or comfortable. Sometimes, walking produces blisters. And blisters, calluses. But life as it is makes you stronger. Walking does too. What adventure will you walk toward?

Think it Out

What are some of the uncommon moments that have come to mind as you reviewed your personal history?

How did it feel to recall these moments for the sake of becoming brave?

How is emotional bravery more or less difficult than adventures like rock climbing, hot air balloon riding, shark diving, etc.?

Can you name an uncomfortable truth that you may have been avoiding?

Can you name a belief that you have proven to be untrue based on the work of this chapter?

Provided that grief no longer holds you back, what adventure will you walk toward? What is your next step?

Feel the Hope

Are you speculating? Are you ruminating? Breathe it out, sing it out, write it out. Make a friendship date—choose a friend who you can and have laughed and cried with. Make a call, share a meal, have a walk, and spend intentional time with the laughter and tears.

Chapter 10: Day One (After D-Day)

"Grief is like a long valley, a winding valley where any bend may reveal a totally new landscape."

~ C.S. Lewis, *A Grief Observed*

We all know someone who is grieving, or has been grieving, the stuff of life other than death. Grieving the loss of a relationship. A friendship. A home. Sentimental belongings. Financial security. Stability. Life as the way you knew it and expected it to be. This kind of grief, the stuff of life, is easily hidden and buried in busyness, shame, and frustration. This kind of grief that walks around in sensible pumps and an unassuming blouse, or parades in the mask of multitasking and achievement, silently gnaws and reshapes the body of the griever. It's that day after the event, the day after the loss, that is scariest.

For She Who Grieves ...

"I was so relieved that I left. It was scary. But I left. My perspective, purpose, and need were focused on survival. I didn't have time to grieve. I had to find a place to live. I had to figure out how to address this with the school. I

needed to buy a car. I can't tell any of my friends what happened; there's too much to do it justice and too much room for misunderstanding and judgment. How am I going to position this and still hold up my values of honesty? The questions flooded and eliminated the space for grief.

"When I was going through my breakup, I couldn't imagine that things would ever get better. 'Where did you go?' This was a hard thing to hear from my friend of forty years, as she looked at me wistfully, slowly shaking her head. 'You are not the You I used to know.' I was so isolated and scared and tired, but I didn't feel safe sharing my grief. Truthfully, I was caught up in survival. If anything, I was grieving the loss of trust in a relationship and in myself. My actions triggered the reaction that ultimately led to our life completely changing. Survival replaced the process of grief. Leaving our family home was not what I imagined. I put my heart and soul into that house. There was so much grief. I didn't have time to grieve those things, I think maybe I was grieving them and didn't really realize it. That grief—it's grieving pieces of yourself.

"In the rare moments when I was free to be with friends and let my guard down, it was still a struggle to release my grief. A friend once said to me, possibly in an attempt at empathy, 'Well, you know, a lot of people go through a hard time when they separate,' which diminished my experience and made me feel worse, while another said a moment later, 'Her life sucks. That's not typical.' I needed to hear that! Thank you for saying that and validating my

experience and noticing the reality that is my life. It is shit!"

When the next day comes, don't overdo it. Don't over-plan it. Don't overthink it. Be present with yourself. Be kind to yourself. Work at healing your unhealed parts and loving yourself. What does this look like? Stillness. But just for a brief moment. Just long enough to acknowledge that stillness is actually a transformative action—the moments of bodily stillness transform and spread through the rest of the body, and the mind. What we do with our bodies helps to move forward the process of the mind, which is important when grief seizes rational behavior, which we know from research that it has the capacity to do! One of those early grief states, shock, requires a bit of stillness.

For some, following the stillness by movement is helpful. Slow, steady, continuous movement. Swimming, biking, walking, hiking. The slow, steady, continuous movement provides a physical avenue for the mind and heart, the internal pieces, to knit together a new blanket of healing and hope. As the mind wanders, lean toward the thoughts that feel best. Continuous motion forward, demonstrating power over the activity of the body, is helpful in transforming the experience.

Commit to stepping forward, and allow yourself to look for an opportunity to be hopeful versus fearful, and disappointed. Start with familiar space, perhaps laps around the neighborhood. Then branch out into exploration when you're ready. Embrace the freedom. It's a new beginning! This action, this habit, is a new beginning in those "days after." Take charge! Seize life, and do it with courage. Engage with the world in challenging ways.

The practicality of the suggested actions might surprise some. It sounds so easy. We are not fools; we know it's not. But it is simple. Putting one foot in front of the other is a way to walk through grief, and it can be done alone or with someone dear. Practice being present, staying in the moment. "If you can concentrate always on the present, you'll be a happy man ... because life is the moment we are living right now" (Coelho, 1995). Choosing to be present in the moment is a direct counteraction to the stage of grief experienced as denial.

Here are more helpful tips from our contributors:

- Just being still. Being present with yourself. Breathing. Just breathing. In through the nose and out the mouth like you're blowing through a straw. Close your eyes. Let thoughts come in and out. Don't fight them; just let them go by; just ignore them. Let your breath move them along.
- Try 5 positive statements to one negative, for example, "I'm pleased with ..." "I'm looking forward to ..." "I like what's happening."
- Take opportunities to be a human BEing vs. a human DOing, instead of constantly reacting. Really, it doesn't have to be perfect. Be OK with OK.
- Consciously choose happiness. Be grateful. Ditch old stories. Find new ones. Take the time to think of the key areas in your life you want to transform. Sit down, and write your new story.

- Get out that journal! Any piece of paper, really. Paper napkins come in handy. Try describing, "What would an ideal day be?" "The greatest day in your life?" Imagine the optimal job, the optimal relationships in your life. What is stressing you? If you were willing to let this be easy, what would you do differently? What choices can you make that would de-stress you?

As a foundation to help people answer questions like, "Am I working and living at my full potential?" "What is my full potential?" "How do I create a clear vision of what I want to accomplish in life, and what legacy am I leaving now and for the future?" Vera Anderson, legacy coach and founder of Global Elements Consulting, mentioned earlier, created an Intentional Legacy Model©:

- **Discover**—Take an objective look at your current state of potential.
- **Declutter**—Gain focus, and take away distractions.
- **Strategize**—Create a simple, elegant, and usable plan.
- **Power Up**—Increase physical and mental energy.
- **Execute**—Apply all the previous steps to practical and sustainable action.

This process can be repeated through every stage of business, career, and life, providing you with a fresh and energizing look at what you are really capable of and steps to get you where you really want to be.

Think it Out

What are my values?

What do they mean?

What is important to you?

What do you enjoy? What does it give you?

What frustrates you?

What are three things that are draining your energy/taking up a lot of your time?

Where/how can you ask for help or remove the responsibility without losing pride, seeming helpless, needy, or irresponsible? And who cares if you do?

What's one little thing you can do to direct you toward your purpose, who you are, and what you want?

Feel the Hope

Take a hike. Really, take a hike. Visit a place that you haven't been before, and discover this difference. Notice. Wonder. That's all.

Try This

Melanie Tonia Evans shared a valuable exercise we've adapted here to help you identify your personal values, what's important to you in how you are treated and treat others, and how you want to experience life. Think first about the behaviors of others that have caused you pain. After listing them, ponder an alternative behavior that you would accept. For example, "Ignored/Dismissed/Avoided" in column one becomes “Listened to/Heard/Considered” in column two. “Criticized” might be “Constructive, caring comments.” You are not limited to five behaviors! Add more spaces as needed.

You’ll start to see patterns emerge and can group themes together however you want, to better give your values each a solid name. Column two is your list of baseline requirements when getting involved with people! This is especially helpful when discerning which new intimate relationships or partnerships are acceptable to you.

List the behaviors of others that have hurt you in your life.	**Reverse each behavior** in the column on the left so it now represents how you DO want to be treated.

Chapter 11: Creating Space

~*~

Serenity Prayer

God, grant me the serenity to accept the things I cannot change,

Courage to change the things I can,

And wisdom to know the difference.

~*~

For She Who Grieves...

"At the time, I was not allowed to tell anyone what was really happening. I didn't even know what was really happening anyway. I do recall wanting so badly to be punched in the face so my wounds would be obvious and I'd have evidence for myself and others of my reality.

"The fact that it was a sudden onslaught of bizarre behavior triggered by my own betrayal didn't help with clarity. I felt guilty and responsible. I was so confused as to why I had gone against my values. I hadn't sought it out, but I do know it was bringing me back to a time when I was a free spirit. I now was partnered, had a demanding job and kid chaos, and despite loving it all, I had a feeling of angst and discontent.

"To add to the confusion, I hadn't ever seen this side of my partner. I knew of their rough past, but I had known them for a long time and we had a solid relationship with lots of love and fun. Had I been blind to treatment contributing to my discontent? Had I missed red flags? I later realized I had seen them, but with my rose-colored glasses, they were an acceptable pink, and I believed in love. Maybe I was just imagining things. I held on to my notion that our relationship was stronger than this, and if I could fix myself, I could fix my partner.

"Meanwhile, I had moved into a separate part of the house, creating a safe-space for myself, with the strict requirement that my "sane-space"—yes, I mean "sane"—was not to be entered; a boundary that was of course, disrespected. This prayer I had scratched on a notepad got me through: 'May I be free of fear and harm. May I be content as I am. May I be at peace with what comes.'

"When I finally realized my efforts were futile and my only valid option was to leave, this prayer got me through: 'If this is for the highest, let it come. Let me be whole with or without this. If not, please protect me.'

"I didn't tell anyone all that happened for a very long time. I lived in silent protection mode. It wasn't always denial; it was just so hard to explain. I could barely understand it myself. But mainly I remained silent because I felt I had to operate in a way that kept me and others safe."

Remember Chapter 3? Abuse comes in many forms. And often with ambiguity. Especially in relationships. So disengaging is not always clear cut.

As we've learned in conversations with friends and through research, narcissistic behavior, for example, in and of itself has many forms, can be exhibited by both males and females, is more prevalent and harmful than one would imagine, and isn't what most people think it is. With narcissistic abuse in particular, it can be difficult to disengage from the relationship because the survivor's cognitive dissonance can be paralyzing (Schneider, 2014). Essentially you had two different relationships with the same person: the lover and the abuser. Two states at the same time in the same relationship, two sets of experiences, two sets of memory about one relationship. Typically we hear the abuse and fear side of PTSD, but in the PTSD of narcissistic abuse, the flashbacks are often the positive, longing rumination of the positive experiences. When experiences of love and abuse are in the same relationship, both sides are linked, but typically, therapists only work with the fear side of PTSD, not the trauma bonding, the dysfunctional connection that forms between reward and punishment.

Some experts who work with people to self-heal after narcissistic abuse and transform their lives emphasize that, to truly disengage from the narcissist, you have to resolve the dissonance to resolve the trauma bond. They also recommend that people experiencing this and desiring healing should seek out a licensed therapist who has experience with narcissistic abuse and understands the dynamics extensively. When people take responsibility for themselves, they don't need to do it all by themselves.

Whether you're dealing with narcissistic behavior or not, you can feel good regardless of conditions you can't control. Think, "My happiness does not depend on what you do. My happiness depends on my own thoughts and choices," and "I love my connection with myself enough that I'm going to maintain it whether I can be with you or not."

For the women in this book and in our larger circle, getting to know ourselves and empowering ourselves in a new reality is, believe it or not, in the end, one of life's greatest pleasures. Maybe it's not what we'd consider a typical joy, but it is definitely a key part of life and incredible growth. Especially when the enlightenment and empowerment stems from trauma or devastation.

As She Grieves ...

"Being uprooted from a new home with no security or support nearby and going through extensive mediations after an intense relationship crisis while working and parenting multiple children takes its toll. Feeling deluded and accosted repeatedly in subtle and not-so-subtle ways in multiple dimensions of my life and having to experience that essentially alone was brutal."

What She Needs ...

"When I moved out, I created a simple sanctuary for me and my children in my new little space. New cozy blankets

for each of us. Comfy pillows. And peaceful, soul-filling rituals for myself that fed my wilted spirit. Every morning, I think truthfully it was for years, after I got my kids on the bus, I would sit on my sofa and just cry. Then, when I could, I'd have a cup of delicious coffee out on the porch to let my pain and exhaustion dissipate into the ether before starting my deadline-driven day."

Remember, where the focus goes is what grows. What you focus on the longest becomes the strongest. Follow what feels good.

As She Grieves ...

"One of my favorite memories is sitting out on the patio of my new apartment, all by myself, looking at my home that was MY choice, and I got to decorate all by myself, the way I wanted to, granted with donations from supportive friends and even friendly neighbors. I loved my cheery curtains and funky chairs and art I had found at an estate sale. I felt so empowered in my own space. I could breathe. Relax. Enjoy. While sitting at my tiny second-hand patio table, I leaned back and actually lit a cigarette, like a celebratory cigar, and smoked it like nobody's business. With a smirk. Just because I could. Just because it was a forbidden freedom, one from my pre-married days. Days when I was young and wild and free. I could now do anything I wanted."

What She Needs...

Making Room for Miracles

Have you ever asked yourself, "If I could invite miracles into my life, what would that look like? What would they be?" Thinking of these things helps form your perspective, guide your next steps and your new life, so you can rediscover yourself and priorities, how you want to live your life, so you can move, no matter how slowly, in that direction. It's OK if it's idealistic vs. realistic. Miracles do happen. And knowing what's important and desirable to you keeps you open to the right opportunities as they pop up and making choices that pave a positive way for you.

It may seem silly, but any of us who have done this know how liberating this is: clean out physical objects that no longer serve you and you don't want to carry into the future—create space for miracles! You don't even have to study the Marie Kondo method!

- Ask yourself: "Does it represent me as I see my ideal self in the future?"
- This could be books, CDs, outdated medicines, broken or cracked items, etc.
- "Thanks for your previous usefulness"—say goodbye with gratitude.
- There are so many ways to do this. Give away one thing a day. Fill a box a day. Shoot for 9 items a day for 24 days! Or pick your own number! Go through one area of your desk each day. One room a day. You'll be amazed how much you can come up with—anything counts!

"Releasing old energy and making room for new was a valuable exercise for me. It wasn't day one after I left my home, but it was a day that I decided I wasn't putting up with residual bullshit that was weighing me down and holding me back. The pandemic shutdown was a great time for this exercise. Or when you are moving homes."

This is also helpful for mental/emotional clutter clearing. *"I created a real Bullshit Bucket where I playfully but powerfully toss anything that doesn't serve me, both figuratively as a visualization and literally, with a satisfying thud. It's the most overflowing—and gratifying—port-a-potty ever."*

"I tried the Japanese method of decluttering where you hold every object that you own, and if it does not bring you joy, you throw it away. So far I have thrown out all the vegetables, my bra, the electric bill, the scale, a mirror, and my treadmill." ~ Internet meme

Release what no longer serves you and gather the scatterings of your soul, the pieces of your integrity that you've given to others, etc. Take back the pieces you've given away—the feelings, emotions, beliefs not accepted by others that are the essence of who you are. Your dreams. Your respect for yourself. Maybe you were hoping to be perfect. Not rock the boat. Maybe you didn't speak up when you wanted to. Pretended you were fine. Open yourself up to the presence of wholeness within you. Respect and preserve your true essence.

Setting Boundaries

In the world of self-help and personal transformation, there is a lot of talk about "boundaries." The word and concept is often misunderstood. There's a difference between boundaries and threats or demands. The intention, respect and compassion, underneath the statement differs. Sometimes it's not black and white. So you have to consider motivation, context, and word choice.

A boundary is something you set around yourself with the purpose of self-protection or self-preservation, when you are motivated to take care of your own situation, and taking full responsibility for your own choices/unhappiness/happiness. "If you continue to abuse me, I will leave," is a boundary. Or, "If you text me harassing messages, I will block your number."

Boundaries are a limit that you set for yourself of what you will accept or not accept, so you can solidify yourself and your values. They do not come from a place of anger, judgment, or blame. Boundaries come from recognizing your own emotional discomfort and serve to inform a person what you will do if the behavior continues.

Threats are motivated by the desire to change someone else's behavior, even if you are convinced whatever you are trying to get the other to do is best for them and for all involved. The motivation there is to force a situation to go your way. When we are trying to change someone else or their behavior through threats or demands, we are not taking responsibility for our own self and our own choices and behavior.

To place a boundary and avoid confusion over interpretation, it's best to communicate it in a way that is respectful and considerate. (By the way, using "please" does not eliminate a threat!)

As She Grieves ...

"My husband asked me, 'At what point are you going to stop letting her wreck you and stop making us pick up the pieces?' I realized my choice to answer her calls was robbing those I loved, and it wasn't fair to them.

"When I say, 'Don't let people rent space in your head for free,' I mean this: The people in your life pay rent for a room in your house (your heart, mind, and soul) ... you occupy their mind/they occupy yours ... people pay for their occupancy ... they pay with their support, concern, etc. When someone calls your phone and you instantly feel your soul is being ripped out, you don't even want to answer the phone. But you wonder, and second-guess yourself, what if something is wrong ... so you answer. And they go right into dumping all their bullshit before even asking about you—not paying any rent. You finally hang up; you're emotionally, mentally, and physically exhausted. Then, for the people who are paying rent in your rooms with their love, support, and encouragement, you're short with them and irritated. That person who called trashed a room in your house, got pissed off, slammed the door, and left. The person/people still involved in your life, have to go clean up that room. These

poor people must deal with the resulting disaster, and that's not fair to them."

What She Needs ...

"It's one of those self-respect things. My husband and I have boundaries for ourselves, our relationship and our home. They are boundaries we created mutually. Boundaries with ourselves, each other, our love, our home that create the stability and happiness we have today.

"Boundaries and discipline. I want to make sure he always feels heard and understood. So especially when times are really busy, we take time to sit in the hot tub and ask, "Are you good?" Check in regularly. "Do you need anything?" One of his boundaries is, "Don't cut me off." He tells me if I am. And I own it, apologize, and move on."

Think it Out

What do you need to release? What has taken your power? Do you need to visualize resentment in a bubble and watch it float away?

What are the pieces you've given away, e.g., feelings, emotions, beliefs not accepted by others that are the essence of who you are?

What boundaries do you need to set to reclaim your personal power?

- Negative emotion is guidance. Let it lead to, "Now what can I do about it?" or "What might I think that's a little more positive?"
- Try, "They did this because they ____. Now what is the gift in this in regard to my own healing, development, and evolution?"
- Instead of thinking about "what they have done or continue to do," focus on, "What is it that *I* continue to think about or feel that is keeping me from being who I really am or feeling good?" Try: "I pledge to take the focus off you and into myself to heal and repair and restore my life force. I declare it is safe to do so because, if I honor me, then all of life will honor me too."

Create Hope

Look for broken things—a great place to start is household goods and the junk drawer. If it cannot be fixed, let it go. Create space literally (and incredibly, internally) by allowing the broken things to be transformed or removed. Start with just 15 minutes, and see what you've discovered.

Part 3

Chapter 12: Finding Hope

Old Grief	New Joy
So tired	Bouncing
Drained	Light
Depleted	Relief
My furrowed brow aches	Fresh air in my veins
Eyelids burn	Sweet soft breeze
The core of my brain won’t stop spinning	Fills my head, tickling
Please be quiet, please be still	My heart
My heart	Is a perfect pink balloon
Has been hollowed out	Laughter
And liquid metal has dripped in	Doesn’t die
I carry a steel weight in my chest	It ripples
All. The. Time.	Under my skin
Please	Reflecting joy
Make it	Like
Stop	The sun

~ Amy Hooper Hanna

~*~

One Good Reason to Hope

After all of this ... the turmoil, the trauma, the tedious work of healing every.single.part.of.it.—we get to make a decision. To hope. We *get to make the decision* to HOPE. What will hope look like now? Are we ready? Will we ever be ready? Is it too late? Is it too soon? What will everyone think? Just find one good reason to hope, and it gets easier.

Guess what. You don't need permission to hope. You only need one good reason to hope. Hope, by its very nature, is based on what is presently unseen. Finding one good reason to hope can build stamina and endurance and remind you that you already have the capacity to not give up. We never said you had to do it all alone. Or by your own merit. Or without the mercy of others. The skills provided in this book and the community that you have access to make it possible to choose hope. Do you want it? Most people who grieve truly do want a reason to hope, even if they can't imagine it. Finding one good reason to hope has now become your *modus operandi*. From sun up to sun down, it is your responsibility to fight for this hope. Hope, realized, is often accompanied by joy. Make joy your job, warrior woman! You're already hired. It's a promotion!

Hope is key to being successful in any grand endeavor; a new job, a relationship, a health treatment. It's a constructive attitude that allows good things to happen and for problems to pass. With hope, you are making an ask to the future, intuitively partnering with what hasn't shown up yet. Hope can be a single ah ha! moment or a power developed by taking steps. It doesn't need to make sense or be supported by hard data, but it can be. Now that hope is your job, and "Joy" is your middle name (laugh if you found the nod here), you can look in the mirror and ask yourself the important question:

How can you tap into your strength to remain positive?

The strength you need is already inside of you. When failure isn't an option, strength will rise from within, and you'll get through it. We've seen it again and again in the stories of the women who have allowed grief to accompany them in this life, who have made hope their job. Here are a few of the ways that hope has anchored them.

When She Grieves ...

"I did one big release; then on holidays like Mothers' Day or at certain events, I might cry for 15 minutes and then move on. Now, I don't grieve the loss of HER, it's the experience of having a mother; the absence of the role. That's a different kind of grief."

"I get to choose to live in the moments and look for hope, capture joy, and choose resilience."

"For me, hope was first found in the realm of affirmations. I listened to a lot of talks on this subject and would write down verbatim the ones that resonated most with me. And I pieced together new ones, like, 'I am healthy, wealthy,

and wise.' I learned it's a skill that needs to be honed by practicing every day with one. Practicing the art of ritualizing affirmations and visualizations and attaching an emotion to it—and acting as if it already happened and what it feels like after it happens. It's a simple practice. The discipline is harder, just because life can so easily get in the way and derail our best intentions. Even something so simple can get sidetracked with life. But the discipline of even carving out a couple minutes a day—just two minutes!—is worth it. If nothing else, it feels good. It puts you in a better place, a better head space. Lets your brain open up a bit, and makes room for positivity."

"I read a book once that said hope is not a strategy. So the word 'hope' is hard for me. For me, it was about boundaries I put up to protect me and my loved ones and my relationship with them. And then, life organically just happened; the boundaries created a life for me that was peaceful; when I put boundaries in place and stuck to them, peace happened organically. My life was peaceful!"

"For me, it has been a private, painful, fascinating journey of slow and steady grief, personal growth, empowerment, and enlightenment."

What She Needs ...

Emotional Freedom

Emotional Freedom, a prominent and dog-eared book used to prepare to share this one, provides more insights on what hope does to a person. Judith Orloff says, "Hope is not blind optimism; it's based on intuition, love, and the gumption to reach the other side [...] more awakened." (2010) We're not talking about false hope, which contradicts intuition and facts. There are things we need to accept and grieve, rather than using hope to enforce our denial. "Sometimes it's helpful to give up hope about a wished-for outcome—painful as this may be—but never to give up hope in the integrity of life's flow, even in the face of great loss."

Did you know that hope amplifies healing by fortifying your neurotransmitters? According to Orloff, hope reprograms your biology and keeps you positive (2010). Being positive increases serotonin and reduces levels of stress hormones. With less stress, you'll feel happier and generally function better. Studies have shown that hope improves the performance of athletes, and that students with great hope of doing well on a test achieve higher scores. Your breathing, circulation, and digestion are particularly responsive to positivity. Hope acts as a natural stress reducer and lessens pain by increasing levels of feel-good endorphins. Take steps (many mentioned in this book) to galvanize your biology with hope!

Part of being brave, in life and most especially as a woman, is understanding that vulnerability is an invitation. Rebecca Dussault, Olympian skier, fitness and wellness coach, and motivational speaker who has been through her own share of challenges, setbacks, and roadblocks shared with a small group of women on a cheery summer day some words that challenged them to look at their own vulnerabilities a bit differently.

The name of the group where she spoke, Brave Women Project, should have given them the hint that her words would be challenging, but when she encouraged them to let hardship and grief galvanize not only hope, but their whole person, there was a resonance that pointed at resilience.

> Claim your story. There's no hiding behind it. None of this, "I can't be this because of that." Know your truth and stand in it. Be bold in your own skin. And guess what? If you want to do things right and well, you will run into red tape. If someone tells you, "You can't do that," just say, "Well, I'll do this then." (Dussault, 2022)

As She Grieves ...

"I felt isolated, lonely, and unwanted growing up with parents who used drugs. I felt responsible. I felt like I wanted to hit the eject button and get out of this situation. I just wanted out of the situation so badly. I did my homework, and started talking to people, to the school counselor; I didn't want to be in that house anymore; I didn't care what I had to do.

"I asked to be emancipated and moved out at 17. I worked three or four jobs, and I'd go to school; at least if I was working, I was doing it my way, with no interference, no one making me feel like shit, no one speaking negatively to me. I would only be affected by my choices, not others' poor choices."

What She Needs ...

"When I went to my high school guidance counselor and said I need out, I need options, he mentioned the alternative school. They were starting a program where I could work a job half a day and attend school half a day. I got to graduate with my classmates from regular school, and it did not make me feel different. My teacher at alternative school was absolutely amazing. She was like a mom to us. She made us feel smart and supported us. I finished all my requirements so quickly that I had the choice to graduate early.

"I learned through all of it that you don't have to use your past as an excuse to be a fuck up today. You have the choice to choose your path regardless of where you came from or what you went through. What I mean by not using your past as an excuse is that you do not have to be a product of your environment. I chose the life I have today. I chose to create the safe, loving life my husband and I have today.

"Without this experience, I would never have known how resilient I really was, nor would I know that I was able to have the perseverance to achieve the life that I have."

According to Viktor Frankl, an Austrian neurologist, psychiatrist, philosopher, writer, and Holocaust survivor, "Suffering in and of itself is meaningless; we give our suffering meaning by the way in which we respond to it" (Frankl, 1992). Having faith in yourself and the power of goodness are attitudes that bring hope to even the harshest experiences. It's extremely empowering when you can turn yourself toward hope. Often, just a tweak in attitude makes a big difference. What we've learned from the women we interviewed was that one meaningful connection with someone who had hope was enough to make it contagious.

Want to be more *x, y,* or *z*? Connect with someone who is that. Look for hopeful people and situations. Hope is contagious. More contagious than HPV, whooping cough, hand foot and mouth disease, and Covid combined. Maybe that's not the most scientific evaluation, but we are pretty darn confident that the affective capacity of hope is significant. So there.

Engage in hope now, engage in The Now, grow as you ought, encourage and empower yourself and others to not just settle, and enlighten yourself to evolve.

~*~

Joy

Joy drinks pure water. She has sat with the dying and attended many births. She denies nothing. She is in love with life, all of it, the sun and the rain and the rainbow. She rides horses at Half Moon Bay under the October moon. She climbs mountains. She sings in the hills. She jumps from the hot spring to the cold stream without hesitation.

Although joy is spontaneous, she is immensely patient. She does not need to rush. She knows that there are obstacles on every path and that every moment is the perfect moment. She is not concerned with success or failure or how to make things permanent.

At times joy is elusive—She seems to disappear even as we approach her. I see her standing on a ridge covered with oak trees, and suddenly the distance between us feels enormous. I am overwhelmed and wonder if the effort to reach her is worth it. Yet, she waits for us. Her desire to walk with us is as great as our longing to accompany her.

~ J. Ruth Gendler

~*~

Think it Out

What is one good reason to hope?

Learning to tap into your intuition—is that where hope lives?

What does hope look like?

Was it ever really gone?

How does a spiritual practice impact mental health?

Will finding hope be easier or harder after the next loss?

What gives you hope? What gives you life? Who? What environment? What calls to you to be the better you?

Feel the Hope

Bring a treat in for your coworkers today, or deliver something to a neighbor. Be the bearer of surprise, and think about the kind of treat that would delight you. Deliver that for yourself next.

~*~

I Prayed for Change

I prayed for change, so I changed my mind.

I prayed for guidance and learned to trust myself.

I prayed for happiness and realized I am not my ego.

I prayed for peace and learned to accept others unconditionally.

I prayed for abundance and realized my doubt kept it out.

I prayed for wealth and realized it is my health.

I prayed for a miracle and realized I am the miracle.

I prayed for a soul mate and realized I am the One.

I prayed for love and realized it's always knocking, but I have to allow it in.

~ Jalāl al-Dīn Rūmī

~*~

Chapter 13: The Return of Devastation

If it doesn't kill you, it might make you stronger.

But it also could make you really mad.

Or determined.

Or depressed.

Or scared.

Or clear headed.

Or ... it's complicated, isn't it? Those waves of grief or devastation just might crash back in, but on the road to hope, something is bound to be found that makes getting back on course a little less impossible.

One of the discoveries made in the writing of this book was the reality of how complicated grief actually is. M Katherine Shear and Colleen Gribbin Bloom discuss treatment of such and explain, "complicated grief is a condition that occurs when something impedes the process of adapting to a loss. The core symptoms include intense and prolonged yearning, longing and sorrow" (Shear and Bloom, 2016).

The work of creating space to grieve can be frustrating and all encompassing. Life gets in the way. At least it can for some. The rapid speed by which one of our storytellers forced herself to experience a miscarriage, which fell days before her 40th birthday, lodged her grief somewhere out there and not where it may have more productively been applied. She came home from the hospital to host out-of-town visitors and a party of nearly 150 people. She wanted people to be around her and felt very much loved and cared for, but she moved on. Quickly. Physically, emotionally, and spiritually, she forced movement. But a year later, the grief returned. Complicated.

As She Grieves ...

"I was wondering why my new job—dream job—just didn't feel right. Nothing was going the way I expected it. I was starting to lose my spark, get down, show up tired, and even cry more. That wasn't like me. There was nothing going on at home or in any of my relationships that had shifted. But then I looked at the calendar, this was when it was happening. This was when I was grieving the most. Or, thought I was. Or should have been. But I stuffed my grief into a 24-hour period and then kept going. Now, a year later, all that bubbled to the surface. And I was leaking it everywhere."

When a person experiences complicated grief, life changes too intensely to process, compounding grief, trauma, and hopelessness. "Acute grief is often intense and highly emotional, dominating our minds and disrupting our lives," (Shear & Bloom, 2016) unless it isn't. Unless there's no time to grieve.

What She Needs ...

Stop the cycle—do that by just standing still.

Name the feeling—look in the mirror and acknowledge what is happening.

Activate your healthy habits—make a choice to do one brave thing.

Put things in order—begin planning for more positive actions to follow.

Yes, that acronym, SNAP, is a great reminder that there will likely be moments of returning to the paralyzing fear or all-encompassing grief. Visually, you may be picturing the amazing moment from *Moonstruck* when Cher yells, "Snap out of it!" (Jewison, 1987). That's exactly what we are hoping for.

For She Who Grieves ...

"I have learned that one's relationship with grief can be lasting and morph over time. Sometimes I can embrace it, other times it barges back in uninvited, just when I think it's finally gone. It can leave and come back, each time showing up in a different outfit, wanting a different relationship with me.

"Usually grief isn't welcome, but if you listen, and let it sit for a while, it's got something important and meaningful to say, in a loving, tender way. In a way, it is telling you the deeper secrets to life."

"If, as a culture, we don't bear witness to grief, the burden of loss is placed entirely on the bereaved, while the rest of us avert our eyes and wait for those in mourning to stop being sad, to let go, to move on, to cheer up. And if they don't—if they have loved too deeply, if they do wake each morning thinking, *I cannot continue to live*—well, then we pathologize their pain: we call her suffering a disease. We do not help them: we tell them that they need to get help."

~ Cheryl Strayed

Think it Out

Is there a word or phrase that you can associate today with how you are feeling about, and in, your grief?

Our work should bring us to a place where we can answer the question, "How has hope grown from this experience of grief?"

What is one piece of advice that you have been given or that you have shared regarding grief that has resonated?

What are you still holding on to?

What comes next?

Feel the Hope

Try a spiritual practice today, or write a poem. We've given you plenty of examples. It may make you a little uncomfortable, or be a joyous return to an abandoned gift. Return or discover, try and do.

Chapter 14: Sharing the Ugly

As humans, we judge ourselves and others more often than we realize. There are positive, neutral, and negative forms of judgment: some of it accidental, some deliberate. Even the way people are, or are not, grieving gets judged. Judging especially becomes a problem when we go out of our way to make unnecessary, hurtful, or unfair judgments and criticisms. Self-judgment is one thing, but sometimes people judge others to make them feel shame or less-than in some way.

Maybe we use it to deflect our own insecurities. We want to know or feel "better than" in some way. Maybe it's careless humor. We may judge out of discomfort, out of fear. We fear being judged. Judgment is essentially about approval and disapproval. Acceptance and rejection. It's plausible that the fear of being judged comes from the need to be accepted, as a survival mechanism from ancient times when rejection from the tribe would essentially mean death.

Fear of judgment can keep us from sharing our realness; it can keep us stuck in grief or prolong the process. Revealing fears, trauma, and secrets is one of the most common environments where people are terrified of being judged negatively. In our perfectly curated social media performance culture, sometimes sharing the ugly is exactly what we need.

And some things cannot be presented on social media. This next interview surprised us, because the grief she carried was so articulate, so colorful, we could grieve with her when she spoke.

Content warning: The following story contains references to sexual and domestic violence. If you want to skip this content, go to the next ~*~ and continue reading.

When She Grieves ...

"There's too much to say, too much unsaid ... is it ok for me to just say it?

"Psychological torture is surreal and insidiously damaging.

"People don't hear much about it. We hear more reference to the overarching term 'domestic abuse.' This has become such a well-known term that people assume they know what it's all about, and they are typically baffled as to 'why the woman didn't just leave?!,' inferring she must be weak or an imbecile.

"Despite being seriously mistreated, sometimes it's not easy, or even wise, or safe, to just 'leave.' This is what I wish people understood before they passed judgment.

"You don't think all that clearly when you are in that situation, you think differently; you are in a dense forest, even if you climb the highest tree and have some perspective, you are still amidst the trees, essentially alone, on a wavering treetop holding on for dear life looking out on an endless forest with no clear borders (and someone stole your trusty ladder).

"Maybe you can't afford to leave because you've been locked out of your accounts; maybe your phone has been taken so you can't communicate easily; you are being tracked and watched so you can't plan an escape. The women's shelter address is a secret for good reason, but you don't know it unless you have a good therapist that ultimately tells you, and it is not easy to find a good therapist and take the time to build that relationship. There are legal issues you can't get your head around, depending on your state there are fault laws that come into play if you are the one to leave, and lawyers cost money, and Googling doesn't get you the truth.

"Maybe you've been threatened that your life will be made more miserable if you leave, and you can believe that because you know how clever and unpredictable they are. Maybe they threaten to tell your family humiliating things about you, and that's your only remote chance of help. Maybe you're guilty of something. Maybe you will have to deal with family and friends, the anger, the doubt. If you have kids, especially sensitive or troubled ones, you might fear it will make things worse in a more complicated/unknown way; maybe you don't want to frighten the children. Maybe you loved this person once and admitting they're abusive is admitting you were a

blind idiot, and you still have hope. Or you think it's really all about you; you just need to fix you.

"They make false promises, so the behavior ebbs and flows, so you think it has stopped. Maybe one day they are back to their 'normal' self, and you have new hope, only to find out some time later that this is not the case. Maybe one day they threaten suicide. Then they say they were kidding. They describe suicide another way another day. Then deny saying it altogether.

"Maybe they have more money than you, are more savvy, and have more connections, so they can get the better lawyer. Maybe not many lawyers know how to deal with narcissistic behavior, especially when it's covert. Maybe you think that many lawyers are narcissists themselves. Maybe you know you will be outwitted, because you can't think in evil, clever ways like they do, and you don't have the energy to anyhow.

"Maybe the person even goes to therapy. So you think they're earnest. But you don't realize they lie to the therapist, because they don't even know they're disordered. They think you're *the one with the problem anyway. YOU are the problem, not them. And their therapist doesn't know either, because this person is a master at deception. Same with the counselor. Because this person is charming and just humble enough that they can't put their finger on the problem either.*

"Maybe physical force isn't involved. Maybe it's coercion, intimidation, verbal threats and waving arms, or penetrating eye stares or rage. Maybe they are standing

over you, clearly angry and hyped, very late at night when you're exhausted, and you are trying to be quiet and reluctantly appease so you don't wake the kids. Maybe they use tactics like constant badgering and long, looping conversations to wear you down, especially at night after a long day, when they can deprive you of sleep and wear you down even more. And you can't prove any of it.

"Maybe they use mental tricks like, 'Show me you love me,' 'You don't seem interested,' 'You're not giving "us" your all,' 'You must not really care,' 'You're not being honest if you can't show me affection,' 'It really hurts my feelings that you won't sleep with me,' 'How can you sleep when I am so concerned about us. You obviously aren't,' 'Seriously you can't stay awake to have sex? I will have to have sex with many others. I'm a sexual being.' 'I have gone without sex to put your needs first.' 'I just want to be close to you.' 'You must not really love me if you won't sleep with me.' 'I love you. Don't you love me?' 'You say you do, but you don't show me.' 'Maybe we need to have more sex. That will improve our relationship.' 'Maybe we need to try different things like role play. Toys. Porn.' 'You want to improve our relationship, don't you?'

"You are in a complicated web that, even if you try to get out, is inherently sticky, and the spider knows the web better than you, because they created it. They even create false hope, and let you twist and turn and wriggle a few bits away. Some days they rest, and let you try to creep away, while other days they come right up behind you and follow your every move. Until they finally decide. It's time. And now that you're exhausted and still and don't even give a shit anymore, although you do, because you

love your babies, you just. Can't. Go. On. So you go numb. And play dead. And hope for the best.

*"And if Fate steps in, someone or something resembling hope comes along and reminds you, 'F*** that goddamn spider! You're a ladybug for crying out loud! Use your unique abilities and fly, lucky lady!' And as Fate would have it, you escape. And you figure it out. And it comes together. And you are at least, safer than you were before."*

~*~

What She Needs ...

Definitely not understanding. It's impossible to understand what she's going through. But standing with? That's absolutely needed.

Patience. It takes a lot of courage to step out of a situation this difficult, and that requires time. Always know there is something you don't know about a situation. Judging carelessly denies people of their truth. It invalidates their grief. Even if they are not there to hear it. The negative energy does not shine a positive light on anyone. Worse, women—very powerful women—so often put the concern about what other people think ahead of their own well-being. We can all do better.

The reality of trauma and grief can easily exist behind the curtain. Judgment and criticism aren't helpful and can thwart the progression of someone processing such pain. It divides. Can we be here to help each other? To share the ugly. To welcome the truth. To validate. To support.

For she who grieves, this is a judgment-free zone. In grief, we are stronger together than alone.

If the words shared in this chapter have struck a chord with you, and you're ready to seek support and help, refer to the list of resources provided.

> Text "START" to 88788, or call 800-799-7233 to speak with someone at the National Domestic Violence Hotline, 24 hours a day, 7 days a week.

Don't wait to be brave enough, let us be brave for you.

Think it Out

Have you been judgmental about the way that someone else has grieved?

What has changed about the way that you think about it now?

Is it really ugly to share grief?

How do you express your opinion without belittling someone else's? How can you disagree without being disrespectful? It matters.

Do you feel like what you're doing is wrong? That question is usually more important than what other people think.

Feel the Hope

Share this book with someone, even if only a screenshot, page, or chapter.

Chapter 15: Brave Enough to Find Hope Again

We're not saying grief is easy to embrace, or that you can look forward to it. No doubt: it's brutal. **We're saying that there are ways to ease the pain, ways to work with it that have a positive impact.** For you and for others.

For She Who Grieves ...

"I was pinned. Pierced. Targeted. Speared in the bullseye of one of those electric dart boards, prized by a professional player. Stuck, but dangling. Alone. Nothing to grab onto. No safety net. I had no choice but to unplug the unit. Sever the connection. Or lose the entire game. I made the decision to pull the plug. I free-fell, plummeting on a paper parachute of hope and will. And I landed. Like a cat with nine lives. Got my feet back under me. Put one foot in front of the other. I re-set myself up for success, in a new spot. Only to have the literal rug pulled out from under me. I had to do it again. Dangle. Uproot. Unsettle. Resettle. And all that landed me in a wiser, wonderful place where I can breathe in peace. In the present. In the moment. Of now. And I know I can handle anything. I am grateful to know my strength."

You may have heard more about "resilience" these days. It's especially a popular term during a pandemic. What is this concept called "resilience"?

Resilience is not grief-resistance. It's not "going numb" or denial. Technically, the definition is about "withstanding or recovering quickly from difficult conditions" and "being able to spring back into shape after bending, stretching, or being compressed."

We promote the notion that resilience is having the strength to come back BETTER. Not just bounce back, but, as resiliency expert, Mj Callaway says, "Bounce-Up™"! Bounce up and over, actually. Rise up and perhaps consider a new direction.

How? Where does resilience come from? Can I buy it on Amazon? Whole Foods must have it!

Is it innate? Can it be acquired? Unfortunately, or fortunately, resilience cannot be purchased. It is a muscle we all have that can be exercised and made stronger and does not even require a gym membership.

Building the Resilience Muscle

When things go wrong, you have to be strong. How do you find the strength? Experience. You build the muscle every time you bounce back. Resilience is developed by experiencing life's inevitable stressors, the ups and downs. That IS life.

We can learn great lessons from entrepreneurs, where resilience is an inherent part of a profession that operates in risk, failure, and renewal. Laura Hitt, owner of Bold Mindset Coaching, organized a free online seminar, Resilience Training for Entrepreneurs, designed to "discover the keys to staying motivated and realizing your vision, and learn to actually love the entrepreneurial roller coaster" (2022). Various entrepreneurs, male and female, spoke of their own experience and work with resilience. Here, we report some of the universal lessons shared by people driven to forge ahead. This all can be applied to handling grief and life's challenges. If you are interested in pursuing any of the ideas in their original context, we encourage you to do an internet search of any of the names provided in our book (see also the References page).

First, reinforcement of a foundational concept: Expect that things will go wrong, and accept that things do go wrong. Success is never a straight line; that's not how life works. Life is not a stable thing. It is not a predictable thing.

A medical and fitness sector entrepreneur, James Webb, suggests a key step he sees people often forget when you get knocked down and get up—*pause and assess before driving forward again.* Be willing to consider a new path or a change that might be better for you (Webb, 2022).

Nadia Ali, a fitness and nutrition coach and supporter of the concept, "If you don't rest, you cannot grow," had a great suggestion for times when you are experiencing a setback or are down, unsure, or unfamiliar: "*The easiest way out of overwhelm is to stop looking at what you have to do and to start looking at what you've already accomplished."*

She also offered this interesting perspective if you are questioning yourself (paraphrased here): *Recognize that everything is energy. You are made of the same four elements of the universe. Water can wipe out an entire island or can simply be sipped. The earth can move a mountain or grow a seed. You get the idea with air and fire. You have that same energy. Channel it. Channel that power. Connect with the elements* (Ali, 2022).

How do you channel it?

Outside of meditating, which is great, how about trust? Trust that the strength is within you. It's within all of us. And take things as they come. Be flexible, like the elements. Look for opportunities to pivot, while staying true to your vision.

The idea of staying "true to your vision" is not just for entrepreneurs. It goes back to the value and importance of identifying your values and the outcome you are seeking—which is beneficial for any of us, in life.

Ask yourself what your goal, your vision, is for yourself in life. You don't get into an Uber without a destination—you don't just let the driver take you for a ride. You tell them where you want to go, and you expect road rules and that there may be traffic. And you want to take the best route.

Knowing where you're trying to get to and what's important to you along the way guides your choices and success in getting there the best way possible. You may not know what the destination looks like, maybe you haven't been there yet. But at least you are consciously moving in what you trust is the right direction.

How do you choose how to pivot? How do you channel your power/strength/energy in the right direction? Ask yourself, does this choice support my main mission? My long-term vision?

Kelli Komondor, visibility strategist and author of *Twenty Won: 21 Female Entrepreneurs Share Their Stories of Resilience During a Global Crisis*, speaks professionally and personally about her experience with impostor syndrome, and agrees that resilience requires vulnerability—our willingness to go deep and be authentic. *"If you can't be honest with other people, you can't be honest with yourself,"* and vice versa (2022). Being vulnerable has a powerful, positive impact. We can be more resilient and stick with our vision, the more vulnerable, honest, authentic we are. We concur.

Merilee Smith, life coach and facilitator of the Ditch Your Drama program, describes the idea of two different mindsets, with two different energies. When we're in the problem-focused mindset, we are in reaction mode, and often take on the negative energy of victim, persecutor, or rescuer roles vs. the higher level, outcome-focused mindset, where we are responding with intention and taking baby steps in what we need to do to move toward that outcome. We create a more empowering dynamic for ourselves when we are operating at this level. This is where we realize growth, evolution, showing up to be better for ourselves and others (Smith, 2022).

You can shift from a negative to a more positive role, move from drama to empowerment, grief to relief, by asking yourself questions like, "What do I want?" or "What is my intention here?" This opens up the opportunity for choosing vs. reacting, building up vs. putting down, sparking growth vs. telling and fixing.

So. Self-acceptance. Accepting where you are. Accepting that you've been down before. And accepting that you have the power and strength within you to shift into a new, more positive state.

Rest and De-Stress

Moving from drama and stress to empowerment and growth is so important to our mental and physical health and doesn't need to be exhausting.

Just like with weight training, progress happens in the action phase, but growth happens in the rest phase. When you slow down, you allow new ideas to form. Self-care gives you the opportunity to acknowledge yourself. If you are taking action and making progress, and making time to rest and grow, you're always going to come back better, because you're stronger.

At the entrepreneur conference we mentioned earlier, Dr. Derek Roger, a psychologist and neuroscientist who has published findings from research on stress and resilience in over 100 papers, as well as books and book chapters, posed the question, "Is there really a good or bad stress?" And posits the answer: "There is not good stress. BUT, it's all in how you define it." "Pressure" is a demand to perform; there is no stress in it. *You can respond to pressure, or churn over stress—it's the emotional upset, the churning, the rumination that is a negative thing.* (Roger, 2022)

When there is constant demand, there is increased rumination and provoking of the fight/flight/freeze response, allowing no room for rest. There is increased arousal to meet the demand. Increased arousal releases adrenaline and cortisol. Adrenaline itself isn't negative. It facilitates action; it's designed to do what it needs to do. However chronic rumination exerts extra cortisol, which compromises immunity. Chronic ruminators have compromised immune systems. And when you're sick, it's harder to be resilient.

Situations, the doctor explained, are neutral. WE turn them into stress (something negative) through rumination. Rumination keeps us stuck in stress, then another event comes along, so we can't get out of stress. Not to mention, once you get into rumination and negative thinking, our self-esteem is affected. While we are not capable of everything, you might want to revisit what you may be undervaluing in yourself, to help you overcome challenges. It's good to both recognize your limitations, and capitalize on your skills.

Remember it's through conditioning that our beliefs are formed as to what we're good at, as well as the negative thinking. People told us things, innocently or not, from our youth that weren't necessarily based in fact that created our beliefs about ourselves and even changed the trajectory of our life. Keep in mind you don't have any less attention or consciousness than anyone else. You may not have the skills of Einstein, that same doctor explained, but we are all born with the same attention and consciousness.

He says rumination is actually a habitual behavior—so you CAN change it. You don't need to stay in victimhood. As for "coping" for example, you can keep your head above water, or you can think that there is just no water. There are people who have developed the habit. To those people, you might say, "Wow, aren't you stressed out? Why aren't you freaking out?" And they say, "What for?" or "What good would that do?" or "Would that really help?"

The doctor used the example of a sleeping cat. What a cat doesn't do is ruminate. When you walk in the room, it is just startled, picks its head up and simply sees it's only you, and lays its head back down to rest. Now admittedly, unlike the instinctive ability of a cat, for us, not ruminating might take some mental practice. As with grief and most of life's most powerful internal forces, as much as we would desire it, there is no magic pill to take care of it.

We dare say there is a magic in the "practice," however. We can become more catlike, in the sense of habitually reacting and releasing, rather than walking around with our fur constantly standing on end.

This will sound familiar: Accept that it exists. Accept that it comes back. Gain perspective. Take steps. Toddler steps are fine. Practice. Persevere. Trust. Know.

The doctor describes four pieces to the practice of building that resilience muscle, which we paraphrase here from our notes.

1. **Stay Here Now**. People are in a waking sleep most of the time. Not present, not in-the-moment. Often we are ruminating about the past or future. Add to that dream the negative thinking, and it's a nightmare. The less time you spend in "waking sleep," the better. Develop an internal alarm to stay in the present. By practicing waking up more frequently, you can practice letting go more quickly.
2. **Control Your Attention**. Notice what's in front of you. This relates to the intentionality of staying in the present, mentioned above.
3. **Become Detached**. This is about keeping perspective. It frees you. See below.
4. **Let Go**. All you have to do is let go, and you're free! This can be the most difficult, because emotion binds us to things. Note this isn't a promotion for avoidance—while in certain situations avoidance for the short term might be helpful, avoidance doesn't work for us in the long term. Avoidance is one of the key inhibitors of resilience, along with rumination.

We like his example of a house, where you are shutting the door to keep the flood out. When held back this way, eventually it breaks through and floods the house. However, opening the front and back doors and then running up to the attic provides a solution. By expressing emotion in the right time and place, you get perspective. Perspective is the key to letting go.

So. Wake up. Control your attention. Gain perspective (Detach). Let go.

What else helps? Sensitivity to others' emotions (this is a learnable skill by the way). And flexibility (picture a reed bending vs. an oak tree crashing in a strong wind).

The best tip: Stop ruminating. You'll be happier!

Reassurance

Shashikala Shanmugasundaram, an architect, author, and senior VP in a male-dominated industry, reminds us that we are stronger than what happens to us. Think about it. The toddler doesn't give up trying to walk because they fall down. We all have an innate will. We all have a powerful energy within us. You CAN do this.

"Always know that you are stronger than whatever life throws at you," she says, *"You've faced setbacks before, and you survived it. If you have faced life before, we can face it in the future"* (Shanmugasundaram, 2022).

So how about shortening the time we stay in a slump? Master martial artist, motivational speaker, and author Dave Kovar relayed several positive points that are part of a mastery mindset, based in martial arts tradition:

- *"If you want to be the best at anything, you gotta be your best."* Make it a point to do the little things to be healthier. You can't do anything, if you can't do anything. Your mental and physical health are everything. When you're sick, it's certainly harder to be resilient.

- "*I can always do more than I think I can.*" Say this anytime you hear yourself say, "I don't know if I can do this." It's true!
- "*I know this challenge will make me stronger.*" Everyone deals with issues. Any of us can look back on any daunting experience in our life and say, "Wow, I got through that." Take the emotion out of the situation, take a deep breath, and take the next step.
- "*I remain calm even in challenging situations.*" This is about developing mental toughness. Try practicing with the little things, like a traffic jam, to build the muscle for bigger things. Think about it. Anger doesn't help you get to where you need to be any faster. But deep abdominal breathing can!
- "*I deflect negative energy.*" When someone spews it at you, realize that it's not about you, it's about them. When someone cuts you off in traffic for example, you can think, "Wow, they're having a really bad day." We are all dealing with our own drama. You don't need to take other's actions personally.
- "*I accept positive energy.*" When someone gives you a compliment, accept it! Simply say "thank you." You don't need to reject it with excuses or self-deprecation. It's a gift! Be engaged in gratitude.
- "*My word is law.*" This isn't being jerky. This is about "I'm going to do what I say." The key to this is setting yourself up for success. Don't demand too much of yourself too soon. Commit to things you know you can do; it will build your resilience muscle! Ask yourself,

> "What can I do TODAY?" Do that for a week, and you've had a successful week! (Kovar, 2022)

There's more to a mastery mindset, and we encourage you to seek out Dave Kovar. We'd also like to include a notion based on a statement by the medical and fitness sector entrepreneur James Webb, that "*Relationships will define your life and fulfillment*" (2022). Developing sincere and genuine, positive and energetic relationships with family, employees, vendors, even competitors, can greatly support your resilience muscle. It's not about introversion or extroversion or a matter of sociability. Even one solid connection or relationship can make all the difference.

The value of connection and relationships was also emphasized by Tiffany Lorraine Galloway, a coach specializing in parent and family relationships who believes that resilience includes self-reliance, self-acceptance and exploration, as well as community. Having experienced her share of life trauma, guilt, and shame, and understanding that humanity is creative and you don't have to do it alone, she created a community of moms.

"*We all have trauma – let's acknowledge that and support each other. We have it in pockets of communities, but where is it in the world as a whole*?" (Galloway, 2022)

Along with music and movement and connection to other moms, she has found that love from her kids propels her the most. She too envisions a future where we embrace life's ups and downs and inevitable grief and are able to step into that power of resilience. Not only accepting what is, but *embracing* it. How can I love this and turn it into an amazing opportunity? Seeing the potential and taking steps to turn the situation into what you want it to be.

Spin a Song

Walk out of your room
beneath the morning sky;
let the sun enter your heart,

and find a way
to keep it there.

Make a song from the light
falling through the air,
and dance even when
you are alone.

Dance if you are still sad.
Dance when you are tired.
Dance until your feet lift
off the ground like wings.

And later, when the stars
are spinning in the night,

put your ear to the ground
and listen to the songs
rising up from the earth

everywhere you go.
There is music.

A poem by Marjory Wentworth, "Celebrating Rumi"
(Alexander, et al., 2017)

~*~

Don't underestimate or undermine how amazing you are. You are more powerful than you realize. You have the privilege of stewarding yourself in this life. Be good at whatever YOU are. Be YOU really well. Start being brave about everything. Ask yourself, what's the bold thing to do here? What you are most fearful of doing is probably a good indicator of what you should do.

Bravery is not fearlessness. Fear is present when courage is demonstrated. Bravery is when fear is surpassed by what you believe is right, important, and necessary. Hope and success are found in moving in the direction toward what you want.

There is magnificence in grief, and courage and splendor in hope and joy.

Life doesn't have to be perfect to be wonderful. Happiness can be born out of hardship. Joy can be born out of grief.

Be passionate about your life and your future. Live hope. It will all be okay.

"I never said it would be easy, I only said it would be worth it." ~ *Mae West* (1940)

Feel the Hope

Wake up earlier this week. Experience the earlier morning hours, even if it's difficult. Use the affirmations and tools in this book to find hope again, and live in that space as much as you can. Are you learning? Are you trying? Focus on what you are doing differently now.

Start early, hope long.

Afterword

I ask her if I can share her story in the book, and she says, yes, with a request that at least for now, it remains anonymous, to minimize impact on her safety, sanity, and privacy and that of others. "To protect my own life? Perhaps. To protect my children's mental well-being? Definitely. To minimize as much fallout as possible when I'm finally feeling good on a new level? Absolutely!

"It really does not matter who I am, other than I am an intelligent, strong, fun-loving, professional person who you might never guess has dealt with this and lived or is living with incredible or enduring grief. I could be your coworker, your friend, the girl next door, your carpool mom, your family member."

What matters is what she experienced and maybe you have too. What matters is that through her story, you learn that you are not alone. What matters is that maybe you haven't experienced this, but now you're more aware of what happens to different degrees and levels even in the most unsuspecting places. Maybe it will spark the education and the empathy our world needs more of. There are so many people out there that you would never guess are going through hell. Be kind to others, and fundamentally, to yourself. Grief responds best to love.

~*~

Majestic

Rise
into the wonder
of daybreak.

Be a rainbow in the cloud.
Be a free bird on the back of the night wind.
Shine on, honey!

Walk with joy in your golden feet
over crystal seas
and purpled mountains.

Know your beauty
is a thunder
your precious heart unsalable.

Be brave,
like a new seed bursting
with extraordinary promise.

Shine on, honey!

Know you
are phenomenal.

Kwame Alexander, “Celebrating Maya Angelou” (2017)

~*~

Practical Wisdom for She Who Moves from Grief to Relief

Grief is not one single emotion. It is a host of emotions we experience over a period of time.

Grief is universal. Also individual. Every person, every situation is unique.

There is no set timetable for grief.

Grief is a process. It can look a little different for everyone.

There is a biological need to process grief.

The process can't be hurried, but it can be helped.

We cannot, and should not, avoid or rush grief, but we can encourage and develop an inner state of peace, hope, and optimism that will help us work with it more easily.

With grief unresolved, hope becomes stifled.

Pain is inevitable, suffering is optional. Choices may be limited, but not lost.

There are nourishing, practical ways to empower a mindset shift that can lessen the duration and ease the intensity of remaining in a painful state.

Some degree of emotional healing is always possible.

Hope and joy can be found even in the darkest of times.

You don't have to go through this alone. Relating with even one person can make a difference.

Objectivity and keeping perspective are important for working with grief.

Self-care is just as important when experiencing grief, or caring for someone who is grieving.

Holding space for grief is critical.

There are opportunities to choose how we deal with grief, hold it, and process it.

One never gets OVER grief. We process it and move forward. And sometimes back.

Embracing our grief, drama, challenge lessens the negativity around it.

Grief is an opportunity for change. Change can be hard.

Leaning into the reality of the change likely better serves us.

Exploring, reconsidering, and reframing our perspectives on grief (as with many things) opens up opportunity and potential to expand our consciousness and live more positively.

A holistic (whole/integrated) approach to experiencing grief and resilience, with a focus on both mind and body, creates the best chance of finding hope, realizing the outcome of happiness, and improving relationships with ourselves and others.

Resilience is fueled by perseverance. Trust. Willingness to change. Exploration. Flexibility. Objectivity. Sensitivity. Vulnerability. Self-reliance.

Our successes are fun, but we learn and grow most from our failures.

Rest, reassurance, and resilience are essential to well-being and manifesting good health.

Intention is powerful. Intention determines outcome. Values define intention. Determining our current values is important.

Grief is complicated. Joy is simple. Hope is the bridge.

What can Help

Hoping for something within reason. Set yourself up for success.

Making time to rest and practice self-care.

Making a personal connection. Relationships. Creating a community.

Asking for help. Try, "I could use your help here." Accepting help when it's offered to you.

Asking for what you want or need. "I want/need" is okay. Advocate for yourself and others too.

Ask someone what you can do for them today. Offer assurance. It feels good.

Acceptance (in many forms). Gaining perspective. Realizing you have choices. Choosing. Taking a step. Even just one step.

There are routines, but you have to find your own thing. We are all unique. There is no right or wrong. Just show up. That's a step.

Having a vision, desiring a clear outcome for your future state. Focusing on the outcome rather than the problem is a place one can find hope.

At the same time, making time to appreciate and be in the present. In the moment. When it feels right, allow yourself to feel what you feel.

Acknowledgment and validation of your grief, understanding and acceptance of the facts, affirmation and gratitude for the positive pieces of your life, recognizing the state you are in and wanting to get to, and support and self-care to get there.

Choosing to live in the moment, look for hope, and capture joy.

Helpful Considerations and Resources

Practices and resources contributors have personally found helpful:

Acceptance and Commitment Therapy (ACT): https://www.psychologytoday.com/us/therapy-types/acceptance-and-commitment-therapy

Brave Women Project: https://www.bwp.life

Cognitive Behavioral Therapy (CBT) and Cognitive Processing Therapy (CPT) Info: https://www.choosingtherapy.com/cognitive-processing-therapy/

Emotional freedom technique (EFT) a.k.a. "Tapping": https://www.thetappingsolution.com/

Eye movement desensitization and reprocessing (EMDR) (Scroll to Info For Laypeople): https://www.emdr.com/what-is-emdr/

Energy work: craniosacral therapy, acupuncture, and Reiki

Free seminars offered by Hay House https://www.hayhouse.com/

Free seminars & articles offered by Avaiya on health and healing: https://www.avaiya.com/about-us/about-us/

My Grief Angels: https://www.mygriefangels.org/

PAAR (Pittsburgh Action Against Rape): https://paar.net/

Post Traumatic Growth (PTG): https://www.apa.org/monitor/2016/11/growth-trauma

Quanta Freedom Healing including Thrive and NARP (Narcissistic Abuse Recovery) programs offered by Melanie Tonia Evans: https://www.melanietoniaevans.com/

Therapeutic coaching and trauma resources:

https://www.alexhoward.com/

https://soniaricotti.com/

https://www.innerintegration.com/

Women's Shelter of Pittsburgh: https://wcspittsburgh.org/

~*~

Crisis Text Line: Text HOME to 741741 from anywhere in the United States, anytime. Crisis Text Line is there for any crisis. A live, trained crisis counselor receives the text and responds, all from a secure online platform. The volunteer Crisis Counselor will help you move from a hot moment to a cool moment.

NAMI Helpline: The National Alliance on Mental Illness (NAMI) HelpLine can be reached Monday through Friday, 10 a.m. – 10 p.m., ET. Call 1-800-950-NAMI (6264), text "HelpLine" to 62640

National Domestic Violence Hotline: Text "START" to 88788, or call 1-800-799-7233. Anyone who is experiencing domestic violence and/or abuse, plus anyone concerned about a friend, family member, or loved one can call the National Domestic Violence Hotline 24 hours a day, seven days a week. https://www.thehotline.org/help/

RUSafe App: RUSafe is a free interactive app for iOS and Android devices that assesses the potential for domestic violence and harm in a dangerous relationship and connects you with nearby emergency shelters and domestic violence hotlines using GPS technology. RUSafe was developed and is maintained by Aspirant, a management and technology consulting firm that focuses its philanthropic resources into raising awareness of domestic violence and supporting victims through its Connection of Hope program.

https://wcspittsburgh.org/partner-violence/rusafe-app/

National Suicide Prevention Lifeline: Call 1-800-273-TALK (8255) or text 988. The Lifeline provides 24/7, free and confidential support for people in distress, prevention and crisis resources for you or your loved ones, and best practices for professionals in the United States.

Acknowledgements

A book wouldn't be a book until we include our heartfelt, sincere, and very special thanks to ...

Jill Hooper and Christina Styers, for your infinite insight and support. Your ideas, your experiences, and your living hope helped shape our voice, and the voices of so many others.

All of the direct and indirect contributors to this book, for your vulnerability and goodwill. Your voices, your stories, actions taken, and wisdom shared are the heart and soul of this book.

Cori, Kelli, and Karen, for your enthusiastic teamwork and professional prowess of the combined forces of Aurora Corialis Publishing, K2Creative, and BetterBeCreative, which brought our vision to reality.

The Brave Women Project community, for your participation and contributions, but mostly for your love and acceptance.

Our dear family and friends, for your love, laughter, patience, interest, input, and care.

You, dear reader, for opening this book and giving us, and yourself, a chance.

And to that and those we grieve, for your life lessons of loss and hope.

Citations for Opening Quotes

Introduction: Lewis, C.S. (1960). *The Four Loves.* HarperCollins Publishers

Chapter 1: Queen Elizabeth II. Brainy Quote. https://www.brainyquote.com/quotes/queen_elizabeth_ii_178865

Chapter 2: Olsson, R. (2020, April 7). *Navigating Grief After a Sudden Death*. Banner Health. https://www.bannerhealth.com/healthcareblog/better-me/navigating-grief-after-the-traumatic-loss-of-a-loved-one-or-friend

Chapter 4: Francois Fenelon, Archbishop of Cambrai, no specific source found

Chapter 5: *What is trauma? - Definition, symptoms, responses, types & therapy*. (2022, June 2). Unyte Integrated Listening. https://integratedlistening.com/what-is-trauma/

Chapter 7: Martin, R. (2020, April 20). *Share Your Poems Of Hurting And Healing*, Poem by Nancy Cross Dunham. NPR, https://www.npr.org/2020/04/20/836950933/share-your-poems-of-hurting-and-healing

Chapter 8 & 10: Lewis, C.S. (1961). *A Grief Observed.* HarperCollins Publishers

Chapter 11: The AA Prayer (Serenity Prayer) Explained. Alcoholics Anonymous. https://alcoholicsanonymous.com/aa-serenity-prayer/

References

Alexander, K., Colderley, C., & Wentworth, M. (2017, March 14) Candlewick Press

Ali, N. (2022, June 3). Resilience Training For Entrepreneurs.

Anderson, J. (2014, March 25). "As the Lights Wink Out." That Jamie: Tales from the Flip Side. http://thatjamie.com/2014/03/lights-wink/

Anderson, V. (n.d.). *Propelling the Power of Your Full Potential.* Global Elements Consulting. Retrieved July 28, 2022, from https://www.globalelementsconsulting.com/

Bifulco, A. (2007), "Traumatic Grief, an Overview." in *Encyclopedia of Stress* (Second Edition), 2007. Retrieved August 3, 2022 from https://www.sciencedirect.com/topics/medicine-and-dentistry/traumatic-grief

Blandin, K., & Pepin, R. (2016). "Dementia grief: A theoretical model of a unique grief experience." Dementia, 16(1), 67–78. https://doi.org/10.1177/1471301215581081

Bonanno, G. (2021, April 10). *Why Some People Don't Grieve.* HowStuffWorks. Retrieved July 31, 2022, from https://health.howstuffworks.com/mental-health/coping/why-some-people-dont-grieve.htm

Byock, I. (2014). *The Four Things That Matter Most: A Book About Living,* (10th Anniversary Edition). Atria Books, Simon and Schuster.

Callaway, Mj. https://www.mjcallaway.com/bounce-up

Christensen, C. M. (1997). *The Innovator's Dilemma.* Harvard Business School Press.

Coelho, P. (1995). *The Alchemist*. Thorsons.

Coelho, S., & Johnson, J. (2022, January 25). *What is Traumatic Grief?* Newport Academy. Retrieved August 10, 2022, from https://www.newportacademy.com/resources/press/traumatic-grief/

Dobler, R., & Wojcik, D. (2017, November 1). *What Ancient.* The Conversation. Retrieved April 26, 2022, https://theconversation.com/what-ancient-cultures-teach-us-about-grief-mourning-and-continuity-of-life-86199

Dussault, R. (2022) https://www.bwp.life/

Evans, M.T. (July 2020). *How To Actually Heal From Abuse.* Retrieved July 15, 2022 from https://blog.melanietoniaevans.com/how-to-actually-heal-from-abuse/.

Fagundes, C. P., & Wu, E. L. (2020). "Matters of the Heart: Grief, Morbidity, and Mortality." *Current Directions in Psychological Science*, 29(3), 235–241. https://doi.org/10.1177/0963721420917698

Fink, G., & Bifulco, A. (2007). *Encyclopedia of Stress*, Four-Volume Set, Second Edition (2nd ed.). Academic Press.

Frankl, V. E. 1. (1992). Man's Search for Meaning: An Introduction to Logotherapy. 4th ed. Boston, Beacon Press.

Freud, S., Strachey, J., Freud, A., & Rothgeb, C. L. (1953). The standard edition of the complete psychological works of Sigmund Freud. Hogarth Press and the Institute of Psycho-Analysis.

Galloway, T.L. (2022, June 5). Mothers Shape the Future summit. Multiple videos. https://www.youtube.com/channel/UC2kptM_tQW491RjV8ZRSNtQ/videos

Gendler, J. R. (1988) *The Book of Qualities,* reissue edition. Harper Perennial.

Gibran, K. (1923) *The Prophet*. Knopf.

Grief and Loss. (2019, November 19). Johns Hopkins Medicine. https://www.hopkinsmedicine.org/health/caregiving/grief-and-loss

Hale, M. [@TheSingleWoman]. (2013, September 5). *Happiness is letting go of what you think your life is SUPPOSED to look like & celebrating it for everything that it IS.* [Tweet]. Twitter. https://twitter.com/TheSingleWoman/status/375608037148749824

Herrera, H. *Frida: A Biography of Frida Kahlo* (1983), p. 197. https://quotepark.com/quotes/1232943-frida-kahlo-i-drank-because-i-wanted-to-drown-my-sorrows-but/

Hitt, L. (2022, June 3). Resilience Training For Entrepreneurs.

Hospice of Southern Maine for our Virtual Thresholds Conference; Grief is Individual and Universal. (2020, May). Press Herald. https://www.pressherald.com/forecaster/forecaster-calendar/#!/details/Grief-is-Individual-and-Universal-VIRTUAL-Thresholds-Conference/10133556/2022-05-10T13

Is it Possible (or Healthy) to Not Grieve? (2020, October 21). Pathways Home Health and Hospice. Retrieved July 14, 2022, from https://pathwayshealth.org/grief-support/is-it-possible-or-healthy-to-not-grieve/

Jaffe, J. & Diamond, M. (2010) *Reproductive Trauma: Psychotherapy with Infertility and Pregnancy Loss Clients.* American Psychological Association.

Jalāl al-Dīn Rūmī. BlogSpot. http://rumidays.blogspot.com/2010/12/sweet-taste-of-grief.html

Jantz, M. (2022, February 8). "Gift of a lifetime." *Mt. Lebanon Magazine*. https://lebomag.com/gift-of-a-lifetime/

Jewison, N. (Director). (1987). *Moonstruck* [Film]. Metro-Goldwyn-Mayer

Keller, H., (1940). *Let us Have Faith*. Doubleday Doran.

Kessler, D. (2019, Nov. 5) *Finding Meaning: The Sixth Stage of Grief*. Scribner.

Kessler, K. E. D., Becker, E., Samuel, J., Kessler, O. E. G. A. G. B. K. D., 978–1476775555, Becker, T. D. O. D. B. E., 978–0684832401, Samuel, G. W. B. J., & 978–1501181542. (2022). *On Grief and Grieving, The Denial of Death, Grief Works 3 Books Collection Set*. Simon & Schuster UK/Souvenir Press Ltd/Penguin Life.

Komondor, K. (2022. June 3). Resilience Training For Entrepreneurs.

Kovar, D. (2022, June 3). Resilience Training For Entrepreneurs.

Leis-Newman, E. (2012, June), *Miscarriage and loss: Losing a pregnancy can affect a woman — and her family — for years, research finds*. American

Psychological Association.
https://www.apa.org/monitor/2012/06/miscarriag
e

Luketic, R. (2001). *Legally Blonde.* Metro-Goldwyn-Mayer Distributing Corporation (MGM).

McFadden, C. (2021) https://www.crystalmcfadden.com/

Miles, J. (2016, July 7). *Understanding Ambivalence and Inner Conflict.* Welldoing. Retrieved July 14, 2022, from https://welldoing.org/article/understanding-ambivalence-inner-conflict

Miles, J. (2017, July 14). "Understanding ambivalence in loss and grief." *Counselling Directory.* https://www.counselling-directory.org.uk/memberarticles/understanding-ambivalence-in-loss-and-grief

Milic, J., Muka, T., Ikram, M. A., Franco, O. H., & Tiemeier, H. (2017). "Determinants and Predictors of Grief Severity and Persistence: The Rotterdam Study." *J. of Aging and Health*, 29(8), 1288–1307. https://doi.org/10.1177/0898264317720715

Moeller, S. (2017, June 22). *Grief: The 40+ Events That Can Be Triggers.* The Grief Recovery Method. https://www.griefrecoverymethod.com/blog/2017/06/grief-40-events-can-be-triggers

Newhouse, L. L. (2021, March 1). *Is crying good for you?* Harvard Health. Retrieved June 21, 2022, from https://www.health.harvard.edu/blog/is-crying-good-for-you-2021030122020

O'Connor, M. (2021, April 22). "The Biology of Grief." *The New York Times.* https://www.nytimes.com/2021/04/22/well/what-happens-in-the-body-during-grief.html

Orloff, J. (2010). *Emotional Freedom: Liberate Yourself from Negative Emotions and Transform Your Life.* New York: Harmony Books.

Phillips, L. (2021, May 4). *Untangling trauma and grief after loss.* Counseling Today. Retrieved August 7, 2022, from https://ct.counseling.org/2021/05/untangling-trauma-and-grief-after-loss/

Pucci, A. R. (2006). *The Client's Guide to Cognitive-Behavioral Therapy: How to live a healthy, happy life... no matter what!* iUniverse.

Roger, D. (2022, June 3). Resilience Training For Entrepreneurs.

Rosenbloom, D., Williams, M.B. & Watkins, B.E. (2010) *Life after Trauma: A Workbook for Healing.* Guilford Press: New York.

Schneider, C. L. B. A. (2014, October 7). *Unreality Check: Cognitive Dissonance in Narcissistic Abuse.* GoodTherapy.Org Therapy Blog. https://www.goodtherapy.org/blog/unreality-check-cognitive-dissonance-in-narcissistic-abuse-1007144

Shanmugasundaram, S. (2022, June 3). Resilience Training For Entrepreneurs.

Shear, M.K. & Gribbin Bloom, C. (2016, May 24). *Complicated Grief Treatment: An Evidence-Based Approach to Grief Therapy*. Springer Science + Business Media

Sheykhet, E. (2020). *One Year After*. Alina's Light Publishing.

Smelser, N. J., Baltes, P. B., Boerner, K., & Wortman, C. B. (Eds.). (2001). *International Encyclopedia of Social & Behavioral Sciences* (1st ed., Vol. 3). Pergamon.

Smith, M. (2022, June 4). https://www.bwp.life/

Smith, M., Robinson, L., and Segal, J. (2018, November 2). *Coping with grief and loss*. HelpGuide.org. https://www.helpguide.org/articles/grief/coping-with-grief-and-loss.htm

Stanaway, C. (2020, June 8). "The Stages of Grief: Accepting the Unacceptable." University of Washington. https://www.washington.edu/counseling/2020/06/08/the-stages-of-grief-accepting-the-unacceptable/

Stern, K. (2019, August 30). *Toby's story*. Rhett Sullivan Foundation. https://rhettsullivan.org/2019/08/29/tobys-story/

Stierwalt, S. (2020, February 9). "Why Do We Laugh?" *Scientific American*. Retrieved June 21, 2022, from https://www.scientificamerican.com/article/why-do-we-laugh/

Strayed, C. (2015) *Brave Enough*. Alfred A. Knopf Publishing Company

Streicher, S. (Creator). (2020). *The Wilds* [Television Series]. Amazon Prime Video.

Trauma and Shock. (2008, June). APA. https://www.apa.org/topics/trauma

Vasquez, J. A. D. (2022, July 21). "Ambiguous Loss Explained: Examples & How It Works." *Cake*. Retrieved June 20, 2022, from https://www.joincake.com/blog/ambiguous-loss/

Villines, Z. (2019, March 14). "Shock and Testing: Two More Twists on the Road to Grief Recovery?" *GoodTherapy*. https://www.goodtherapy.org/blog/shock-testing-two-more-twists-on-road-to-grief-recovery-0314197

Walsch, N. D. (1995) *Conversations with God, An Uncommon Dialogue: Living in the World with Honesty, Courage, and Love - Volume 1*. Berkley

Webb, J.H. (2022, June 3). Resilience Training For Entrepreneurs.

West, M. (1940). *The Constant Sinner*. Sheridan House

Wollerton, M. (2022, March 5). https://www.bwp.life/

Yearning Most Salient Feeling Following a Loss (Feb 20, 2007). Yale School of Medicine. https://medicine.yale.edu/news-article/yearning-most-salient-feeling-following-a-loss/

About the Authors

Ms. Amy Hooper Hanna serves as a coach, trainer, and consultant in employee communication and engagement and leadership effectiveness. She consulted with Fortune 500 and Fortune 1000 companies in organization effectiveness and communications for more than a decade in a leading human capital firm in Washington D.C., then spent another decade with a leading talent management firm, assessing corporate client leadership behavior and providing developmental feedback.

In between, soon after she became a mom (another key role) for the second time, she established her own independent entity, Amy Hooper Hanna & Associates (AhHA!), which started as a strategic employee research consultancy for employee engagement, retention, communications and marketing projects, and has since shifted focus to leadership coaching, making people-leadership easier with practical wisdom that works. As a strategist, researcher, communicator and coach, she asks questions and listens closely in both life and business, creating "ah ha!" moments for people that generate positive momentum. As a single mom of three, she simply takes the approach of "AHHH!"

Amy encourages taking a leap of faith and trusting oneself and life, while questioning it too. She created the work flexibility she needs to responsibly be who she wants, and continues to take risks to consciously carve out the "shoulds" and commit to what feels intuitively and intellectually right and light, to live a life of meaning and positive, personal impact.

Noted for being unflappable in the face of life's constant blows, her grace (ha!) under pressure, and for seeing the humor in the most absurdly horrible, Amy is a big believer in laughter, learning, and happy hour. She admittedly dislikes meanness and dog poop.

With family roots in writing and publishing, Amy is proud to produce her first book! She is also working on *Soul Snippets for the Kiddos*, a legacy collection of treasured insights she has noted over the years. She is so excited to be on this adventure of life with you and honored to partner with Holly on *For She Who Grieves: Practical Wisdom for Living Hope*.

Ms. Holly McIlwain, M.S., is the founder and chief cheerleader of the Brave Women Project. As an author, Holly dreams of telling stories that matter. Her first book, *For She Who Leads: Practical Wisdom from a Woman Who Serves*, was published in 2020. She also is a contributing author in the anthology *Twenty Won: 21 Female Entrepreneurs Share Their Stories of Business Resilience During a Global Crisis*, which is an Amazon bestseller and was published in April of 2021.

Professionally, Holly leads the Talent Development platform at Winner Partners. She is a subject-matter expert in the usage of behavior assessments as part of coaching and development plans, in addition to talent acquisition engagements. As a Gallup Certified Strengths Coach, working with individuals and organizations to build a better world and sustainable business solutions is her passion. What's not exciting about that? This enthusiasm comes with Holly into each coaching session, team workshop, search opportunity, and speaking engagement. It carries right over into the Brave Women Project. Nothing excites Holly more than inspiring women to do brave things.

Developing leaders who change lives is Holly's passion and professional purpose. She has studied and written about topics such as leadership and mission, bravery in business, and managing human relationships. As a recognized subject matter expert, Holly has spoken at numerous conferences and on Sirius XM Radio. She holds an advanced degree in Organizational Leadership from Robert Morris University and is certified as a DISC Behavior Analyst and a Driving Forces Behavior Analyst.

After studying with Pittsburgh Leadership Foundation, she invested her time and professionalism in the Pittsburgh region, consistently seeking ways to challenge leaders to become fully engaged in transformation. In 2020 she served as Pittsburgh Leadership Foundation faculty and became a DDI-certified facilitator. Holly is an expert in the value of dynamic onboarding as part of the foundation for fully engaged employees and was the director of human resources and talent management at Robert Morris University. Currently, she is lending those talents to her undergraduate alma mater, Franciscan University.

Holly invests herself to expand the reach of those organizations she serves and has a long record of engagement in the region. Holly functioned as a lead consultant in organizational management and leadership

CPSIA information can be obtained
at www.ICGtesting.com
Printed in the USA
BVHW030820131122
651490BV00006B/18